First Edition of the Workshop on Scaling Behavior of Large Language Models (SCALE-LLM 2024)

St. Julian's, Malta
22 March 2024

ISBN: 978-1-7138-9459-9

Printed from e-media with permission by:

Curran Associates, Inc.
57 Morehouse Lane
Red Hook, NY 12571

Some format issues inherent in the e-media version may also appear in this print version.

Printed with permission by Curran Associates, Inc. (2025)

Association for Computational Linguistics
209 N. Eighth Street
Stroudsburg, Pennsylvania 18360

Phone: 1-570-476-8006
Fax: 1-570-476-0860

acl@aclweb.org

Additional copies of this publication are available from:

Curran Associates, Inc.
57 Morehouse Lane
Red Hook, NY 12571 USA
Phone: 845-758-0400
Fax: 845-758-2633
Email: curran@proceedings.com
Web: www.proceedings.com

SCALE-LLM 2024

First edition of the Workshop on the Scaling Behavior of Large Language Models (SCALE-LLM 2024)

Proceedings of the Workshop

March 22, 2024

The SCALE-LLM organizers gratefully acknowledge the support from the following sponsors.

Platinum

Google

Silver

Meta

Organizers' personal sponsors

UKRI Research Node on TAS Governance & Regulation

Apart

Association for Computational Linguistics (ACL)
209 N. Eighth Street
Stroudsburg, PA 18360
USA
Tel: +1-570-476-8006
Fax: +1-570-476-0860
acl@aclweb.org

Introduction

We are excited to welcome you to SCALE-LLM 2024, the First Workshop on the Scaling Behavior of Large Language Models. SCALE-LLM 2024 is being held in Malta on 22 March 2024, co-located with EACL 2024.

The purpose of this workshop is to provide a venue to share and discuss results of investigations into the scaling behavior of Large Language Models (LLMs). We are particularly interested in results displaying interestingscaling curves (e.g., inverse, u-shaped, or inverse u-shaped scaling curves) for a variety of tasks. These results, where the performance of the LLMs decreases with increasing model size or follows a non-monotonic trend, deviating from the expected the bigger, the betterpositive scaling laws, are of great scientific interest as they can reveal intrinsic limitations of current LLM architectures and training paradigms and they provide novel research directions towards a better understanding of these models and of possible approaches to improve them.

Recently, there has been an increasing interest in these phenomena from the research community, culminating in the Inverse Scaling Prize, which solicited tasks to be systematically evaluated according to a standardized protocol in order to perform a systematic study. The SCALE-LLM Workshop will expand these efforts. In contrast to the Inverse Scaling Prize, which focused on zero-shot tasks with a fixed format, we are also interested in, for example, few-shot and alternate prompting strategies (e.g. Chain-of-Thoughts), multi-step interactions (e.g. Tree-of-Thoughts, self-critique), hardening against prompt injection attacks (e.g. user input escaping, canary tokens), etc.

The program includes two keynote talks, three oral presentations, a discussion panel and a poster session.

We extend special thanks to our Program Committee members, our Keynote speakers Najoung Kim and Ian McKenzie, the EACL workshop chairs Nafise Moosavi and Zeerak Talat, the publication chairs Danilo Croce and Goezde Guel Sahin and all the EACL organizers.

We thank our Platinum sponsor Google Research, our Silver Sponsor Meta and our organizers personal sponsors UKRI Research Node on Trustworthy Autonomous Systems Governance and Regulation (for Antonio Valerio Miceli-Barone) and Apart Research (for Fazl Barez). Thanks to the generosity of our Platinum sponsor Google Research we are able to provide a monetary prize for our best paper award and provide financial aid to student presenters.

The SCALE-LLM 2024 organizers

Antonio Valerio Miceli-Barone, Fazl Barez, Shay B. Cohen, Elena Voita, Ulrich Germann, Michal Lukasik

Organizing Committee

Workshop Organizers

Antonio Valerio Miceli-Barone, University of Edinburgh
Fazl Barez, University of Oxford
Shay B. Cohen, University of Edinburgh
Elena Voita, Meta
Ulrich Germann, University of Edinburgh
Michal Lukasik, Google Research

Program Committee

Reviewers

Ernest Davis

Marcio Fonseca

Ulrich Germann, Adam Grycner, Sarang Gupta

Barry Haddow, Jacob Hilton

Najoung Kim

Shihao Liang

Ian R. McKenzie, Antonio Valerio Miceli-Barone

Alicia Parrish

Parth Sarthi

Lucas Torroba Hennigen

Yftah Ziser

Keynote Talk

Inverse Scaling: When Bigger isn't Better

Ian McKenzie
OpenAI (contractor)
2024-03-22 09:45:00 – Room: **Fortress 1**

Abstract: Work on scaling laws has found that large language models (LMs) show predictable improvements to overall loss with increased scale (model size, training data, and compute). I'll discuss the phenomenon of inverse scaling": that LMs may show worse task performance with increased scale, e.g., due to flaws in the training objective and data. We collected empirical evidence of inverse scaling on 11 datasets collected by running a public contest, the Inverse Scaling Prize. Through analysis of the datasets, along with other examples found in the literature, we identified four potential causes of inverse scaling: (i) preference to repeat memorized sequences over following in-context instructions, (ii) imitation of undesirable patterns in the training data, (iii) tasks containing an easy distractor task which LMs could focus on, rather than the harder real task, and (iv) correct but misleading few-shot demonstrations of the task. Our tasks have helped drive the discovery of U-shaped and inverted-U scaling trends, where an initial trend reverses, suggesting that scaling trends are not always monotonic and that existing scaling laws less reliable at predicting the behavior of larger-scale models than previously understood. Our results suggest that there are tasks for which increased model scale alone may not lead to improved performance, and that more careful thought needs to go into the data and objectives for training language models.

Bio: Ian McKenzie is the main organizer of the Inverse Scaling Prize and first author of the associated paper, currently he is a contracting Research Engineer on OpenAI's Dangerous Capability Evaluations project.

Keynote Talk

Najoung Kim
Boston University / Google
2024-03-22 14:30:00 – Room: **Fortress 1**

Abstract: to be decided

Bio: Najoun Kim is an Assistant Professor at Boston University and a researcher at Google. She is also one of the authors of the Inverse Scaling Prize paper as well as other foundational works in this field.

Table of Contents

Program

Friday, March 22, 2024

09:00 - 09:15 *Opening Remarks*

09:15 - 09:45 *Invited Talk 1 - Ian McKenzie*

09:45 - 10:30 *Oral presentations*

Scaling Behavior of Machine Translation with Large Language Models under Prompt Injection Attacks
Zhifan Sun and Antonio Valerio Miceli-Barone

InstructEval: Towards Holistic Evaluation of Instruction-Tuned Large Language Models
Yew Ken Chia, Pengfei Hong, Lidong Bing and Soujanya Poria

When do Generative Query and Document Expansions Fail? A Comprehensive Study Across Methods, Retrievers, and Datasets
Orion Weller, Kyle Lo, David Wadden, Dawn J Lawrie, Benjamin Van Durme, Arman Cohan and Luca Soldaini

10:30 - 14:00 *Break*

14:00 - 14:30 *Invited talk 2 - Najoung Kim*

14:30 - 15:15 *Panel discussion*

15:15 - 15:30 *Best paper announcement and closing remarks*

15:30 - 17:30 *Poster session*

A Proposal for Scaling the Scaling Laws
Wout Schellaert, Ronan Hamon, Fernando Martínez-Plumed and Jose Hernandez-Orallo

Scaling Behavior of Machine Translation with Large Language Models under Prompt Injection Attacks
Zhifan Sun and Antonio Valerio Miceli-Barone

Can Large Language Models Reason About Goal-Oriented Tasks?
Filippos Bellos, Yayuan Li, Wuao Liu and Jason J Corso

Friday, March 22, 2024 (continued)

InstructEval: Towards Holistic Evaluation of Instruction-Tuned Large Language Models
Yew Ken Chia, Pengfei Hong, Lidong Bing and Soujanya Poria

Detecting Mode Collapse in Language Models via Narration
Sil Hamilton

When do Generative Query and Document Expansions Fail? A Comprehensive Study Across Methods, Retrievers, and Datasets
Orion Weller, Kyle Lo, David Wadden, Dawn J Lawrie, Benjamin Van Durme, Arman Cohan and Luca Soldaini

A Proposal for Scaling the Scaling Laws

Wout Schellaert[1,2] **Ronan Hamon**[3] **Fernando Martínez-Plumed**[1]

José Hernández-Orallo[1,2]

[1]Valencian Research Institute for Artificial Intelligence (VRAIN), Universitat Politècnica de València
[2]Leverhulme Centre for the Future of Intelligence, University of Cambridge
[3]European Commission, Joint Research Centre, Ispra, Italy
wschell@vrain.upv.es

Abstract

Scaling laws are predictable relations between the performance of AI systems and various scalable design choices such as model or dataset size. In order to keep predictions interpretable, scaling analysis has traditionally relied on heavy summarisation of both the system design and its performance. We argue this summarisation and aggregation is a major source of predictive inaccuracy and lack of generalisation. With a synthetic example we show how scaling analysis needs to be *instance-based* to accurately model realistic benchmark behaviour, highlighting the need for richer evaluation datasets and more complex inferential tools, for which we outline an actionable proposal.

1 Introduction

Analysing how AI systems *scale* – how their performance is affected by various design choices such as parameter count or dataset size – has become a fruitful empirical tool: it informs the design of new generations of (scaled-up) systems (Hoffmann et al., 2022), uncovers architectural limitations (McKenzie et al., 2023), and generally helps both industry and policy in planning for what the near future of AI might look like. For example, the concept of *scaling laws* (Hestness et al., 2017; Villalobos, 2023) deals with capturing predictable patterns in the relation between scale and performance into simple mathematical relations, from which data driven extrapolations and predictions about next-generation performance can then be made.

Despite the usefulness of scaling analysis, there are also several issues. A primary concern is generalisation. Scaling laws need to be tailored (i.e. fitted) to different domains, architectures, and often even to each set of model hyperparameters independently. There is no universal 'scaling law' (Abnar et al., 2021; Caballero et al., 2022). Insights that generalise across tasks and metrics are rare. A second notable issue is predictive accuracy. For example, modelling breakpoints – changes in the behavioural trend – has proven difficult, partly because of the limited expressivity of the functional forms (Caballero et al., 2022), but also because new capabilities seemingly emerge out of the blue at certain scales (Wei et al., 2022)[1].

We argue that *oversummarisation* is a significant contributing factor to these issues. Firstly, the dimensions of scale and size capture only a small part of technological innovation, and are a rudimentary summary of the attributes that define and differentiate AI systems overall. Current methods typically consider only one or two scalable design choices. This is the **oversummarisation of systems**.

Secondly, the empirical aggregate performance metrics that act as the unit of analysis are, by construction, summary statistics. By not looking at the actual features of the task instances – like a researcher might – performance is treated as an abstract number, devoid of information that could explain differences. The detection of patterns underlying the relation between task features, system features, and performance is off the table from the start. For example, the aggregate metrics cannot capture any difference in scaling behaviour between subsets of the benchmark. This is the **oversummarisation of task performance**.

While this heavy summarisation is sensible in the light of interpretability or data scarcity, it comes at a cost of generalisation and predictive power. With major NLP evaluation efforts like BIG-Bench (Srivastava et al., 2022) and HELM (Liang et al., 2022) producing huge quantities of instance-level evaluation results across a plethora of different AI systems, it is time to capitalise on the available data, and much like we scale AI itself, to also *scale the inferential tools we use in our analysis of AI.*

[1]Schaeffer et al. (2023) convincingly argue that this is due to the bluntness of the used metrics.

Proceedings of the First edition of the Workshop on the Scaling Behavior of Large Language Models, pages 1–8
March 22, 2024

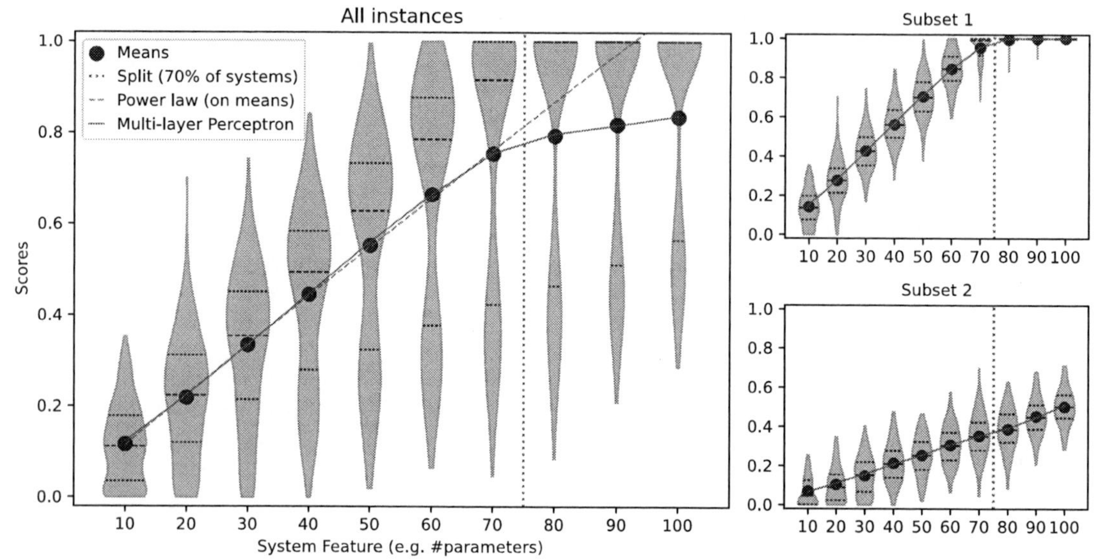

Figure 1: Synthetic example of task performance correlating with system scale which cannot be modelled from aggregate measures, while being completely regular from an instance-level perspective. The plot shows ten synthetic AI systems, whose synthetic evaluation scores are designed to be dependent on an abstract feature of the system. For example, system 2 has feature-value 20 (e.g. number of parameters), and has a mean score of about 0.2. The violin plots, with the quantiles marked, represent the distribution of scores of the respective systems. The red line is a power law fitted to the mean scores, while the blue line represents the aggregated predictions of a simple multi-layer perceptron (MLP) that predicts instance level scores. Both are trained/fitted on the smallest seven systems only. The last three systems then act as a test for the performance predictor.

2 Synthetic Example

To illustrate the challenges outlined earlier and to lay the foundation for our proposed methodology, we present a synthetic scenario where the scaling behaviour cannot be modelled from aggregate measures. The setup is as follows: we hypothesise ten AI systems, each of which scales up over the same (abstract) system feature, e.g. number of model parameters. We also devise a simple synthetic dataset consisting of 1000 instances divided into two subpopulations. The instances of the dataset synthetically have only one feature: a one-hot coded vector indicating which of the two different subgroups of the benchmark the instance belongs to.

To bring this to life, consider the task of sentiment classification of English text, whose domain would naturally contain a blend of English varieties, e.g. 'standard English', acting as subpopulation 1, and African-American Vernacular English (AAVE), acting as subpopulation 2. In this scenario, a one-hot vector indicating the subpopulation would not be provided explicitly, but actual features of the English variants would allow identifying the texts as belonging to different populations.

We now generate synthetic evaluation results, where we design the scores to be dependent on the scalable system feature. We simply let the mean score increase as the system feature scales. We also make this relation between scale and score differ between the two subpopulations, e.g. the sentiment of AVEE might be harder to classify than that of standard English, for example due to lower representation in training data. The scores are in the range $[0, 1]$, representing e.g. the probability assigned to the correct class.

Figure 1 illustrates the example. Observing only the mean scores, a conventional scaling analysis could sensibly only make a linear extrapolation (in red). On the other hand, an instance-based approach could discern the distinct subpopulations, noting that performance must saturate in the first group while increasing more gradually in the second. To exemplify this, we train a simple neural network[2] on the set of synthetic evaluation records[3] to predict instance-level scores, that can correctly extrapolate to larger systems (blue curve).

[2]A scikit-learn MLPRegressor with default parameters, with outputs clipped between 0 and 1.

[3]Tuples $\langle$system feature, instance feature, score$\rangle$.

Evaluation Records			
System Features (id, #params, #tokens)	**Instance Features** (same as the systems gets)	Model Outputs (optional)	**Score** (number)
GPT4, 1.8T, 2T	What movie do these emojis represent?		1
GPT4, 1.8T, 2T	Translate "Can I have the bill please?" into Italian.		0.7
Bard, 350G, 1.5T	What movie do these emojis represent?		0
...	...		...

Figure 2: Example dataset of evaluation records.

While the example is obviously exaggerated and idealistic, benchmark subgroups are not uncommon (Swayamdipta et al., 2020; Siddiqui et al., 2022). In a high-dimensional problem space like NLP, the subgroups are however not as crisp as in our example, and identifying them is far from straightforward; this complexity is precisely why we need more sophisticated statistical methods beyond simple aggregate measures. In general, it is hard to isolate a single capability in benchmark design (AREA et al., 2014; Hernández-Orallo, 2017), if that even makes sense for novel kinds of intelligence like LLMs. In reality, there will be a mixture of (meta-)features of both system and instance that influence the scores in complicated ways. Example instance features that the literature has shown to be impactful are input length or grammatical complexity (Graesser et al., 2011; Kazemnejad et al., 2023); Clever Hans phenomena and general confounding (Martínez-Plumed et al., 2022); mislabelling (Northcutt et al., 2021; Kreutzer et al., 2022), label disagreement (Aroyo and Welty, 2015; Pavlick and Kwiatkowski, 2019), or task ambiguity (Liu et al., 2023); or general dependence on other skills, e.g. for dealing with numeric values (Amini et al., 2019), negation (She et al., 2023), or social understanding (Sap et al., 2019). While these phenomena are also tested for individually, they are nonetheless confounding factors in most benchmarks. They influence scaling behaviour in currently unknown ways and require us to actually relate scores to instance features, instead of treating performance as an abstract number.

3 Proposal

Our proposed approach emphasises the integration of detailed evaluation data. It involves following three-step process:

1. **Collect a dataset of evaluation records**, where each record corresponds to the score a particular AI system achieved for a particular task instance. The dataset can incorporate multiple tasks and multiple systems, and preferably does so in order to enable cross-system and cross-capability generalisation. While it is unfortunately rare to make fine-grained evaluation data publicly available (Burnell et al., 2023), recent evaluation efforts such as BIG-Bench (Srivastava et al., 2022) and HELM (Liang et al., 2022) have made massive amounts of instance-level scores available that can be adopted directly. At the same time, one should describe the systems under examination with machine-readable features, which can range from straightforward attributes like model size to complex architectural characteristics or whether specific training methods such as RLHF (Ouyang et al., 2022) were used. Any design choice that plausibly has significant impact on performance is useful and needed information. Figure 2 illustrates an example of such a dataset.

2. **Train an instance-level score predictor.** Hernández-Orallo et al. (2022) introduced assessor models as conditional density estimators $\hat{p}(r|\pi, \mu)$ for doing predictive inference regarding score r given system features π and instance μ. Starting from the dataset of evaluation records, the estimator $\hat{p}(r|\pi, \mu)$ can be constructed as a standard machine learning system, with π and μ acting as inputs, and score r acting as the label. For our sentiment classification for example, it could be a regression tree trained from tabular system feature data and embeddings of the textual instances.

3. **Predict scores for hypothetical systems.** Equipped with the predictor $\hat{p}(r|\pi, \mu)$, we can describe a hypothetical system π' –with scaled up features– and collect instance-level score predictions for the instances of existing benchmarks. To make an overall performance estimation for π' on a benchmark dataset D, we simply combine the individual predictions, for example by averaging the predicted score for each instance in D: $1/|D| \sum_{\mu \in D} \arg\max_r \hat{p}(r|\pi', \mu)$ – analogous to how we would compute actual scores.

The design space for assessor models is large and the inferential problem is still a challenging extrapolating one. But the approach we propose should be able to – with the right inductive biases – at least equal the predictive accuracy of current scaling law methods since the same (and more) information is used. It can capture nonlinear behaviour before aggregation, and with appropriate design, generalisation and predictive accuracy should improve over low dimensional methods.

Apart from the pure predictive aspect, this approach can provide other scaling related insights as well. For example, one could use feature attribution methods to decouple the influence of various (scaled-up) design choices, comparing e.g. influence of scaling human feedback versus scaling the causal next-token training. One could reverse engineer the design of GPT-4 (OpenAI, 2023) by searching for the features that most accurately match actual GPT-4 performance. And while we have focused on extrapolation, it is perfectly possible to ask interpolating questions, e.g. investigating the performance trade-offs and identifying "sweet spots" for system design – such as the mix of training data, the type of optimisation algorithm used, or the inclusion of certain features – that stick to more familiar territory.

4 Related Work

Scaling laws in deep learning research focus on empirical relationships between performance metrics and design choices such as architecture, model size, or dataset size. Initially driven by findings that test loss scales with training data size in a power-law fashion (Hestness et al., 2017), research has diversified to analyse a range of tasks and architectures (Rosenfeld et al., 2019; Henighan et al., 2020; Kaplan et al., 2020) and to theorise scaling exponents (Sharma and Kaplan, 2020; Hutter, 2021; Bahri et al., 2021). However, recent work highlights the non-universal applicability of these laws, particularly in predicting downstream task performance (Hoffmann et al., 2022; Sorscher et al., 2023; Caballero et al., 2022), which is further complicated by the nuances of transfer learning (Abnar et al., 2021; Tay et al., 2022). In general, we find a critical gap in current methods: the over-reliance on aggregated data and limited system characteristics.

Approaches that deal with oversummarization of systems are proposed by Srinivasan et al. (2022) and Jain et al. (2023), which learn or meta-learn from multiple system features and therefore generalise better across systems and tasks, but still work at the aggregate performance level.

Instance-level score prediction is closely related to the notion of predictive uncertainty and calibration in probabilistic systems. Including for LLMs, it revolves around the idea that these systems can signal their own confidence by assigning probabilities to potential outcomes, much as we expect from evaluative models. Predictive uncertainty is the focus of intense research (Mielke et al., 2022; Kadavath et al., 2022; Baan et al., 2023; Hu et al., 2023), but conclusions are often contradictory or context dependent. The fields of anomaly detection and confidence estimation (e.g. Corbière et al., 2019 and Qu et al., 2022) are closely related as well. As described by (Hernández-Orallo et al., 2022), these investigations typically assume requirements that make them differ from the pure 'performance prediction' perspective adopted in our approach, e.g. by not being anticipative and requiring access to model outputs or internals, both of which are not available in the context of scaling laws.

The performance prediction idea also extends and is influenced by other research areas, such as Item Response Theory (Martínez-Plumed et al., 2019; Vania et al., 2021), which predicts success based on system ability and task difficulty, and techniques such as surrogate evaluation (Sacks et al., 1989) and Datamodels (Ilyas et al., 2022), which examine model behaviour in relation to training data. In addition, methods for detailed error analysis (Amershi et al., 2015) contribute to the understanding of model performance by identifying incorrect predictions and highlighting strengths and weaknesses.

5 Conclusion

Acknowledging the challenges of scaling analysis, our proposal aims to mitigate them by leveraging a richer dataset and more powerful inferential tools, i.e. "scaling the scaling laws". The approach unlocks various new applications and aspires to enhance predictive accuracy and generalisation, ultimately aiming for a single assessor model doing inference about scaling behaviour for all tasks and systems with sufficient evaluation data available. We invite the research community to contribute to this endeavour by harnessing instance-level evaluations and amplifying the collective progress in understanding AI performance.

Limitations

While our approach aims to help remediate the challenges of scaling analysis, it of course does not wholly fix the problems of generalisation and predictive accuracy in such a complex and multidimensional extrapolation setting. Predicting non-linear performance trends requires careful assumption making, especially when no trend reversal has been observed. Feature engineering is also critical, but is complicated by mixed input types, label imbalance, unknown variables, inconsistencies and noisy data. The large design space requires strategic decisions about model training and data handling, presenting us with a challenging machine learning problem, compounded by the conventional perils of scaling analysis.

Ethics Statement

We acknowledge the ethical responsibilities inherent in predicting AI scalability and are committed to transparency and the cautious application of our models. While we aim to inform resource allocation and research direction, we urge against overreliance on predictions for critical decisions and emphasise the importance of safety, fairness, and mitigating potential risks as AI systems advance. Any forecast made by our approach should be interpreted as a rough estimation, not as the definite path forward.

Acknowledgements

This work was funded by valgrAI, the Norwegian Research Council grant 329745 Machine Teaching for Explainable AI, the Future of Life Institute, FLI, under grant RFP2-152, CIPROM/2022/6 and IDIFEDER/2021/05 (CLUSTERIA) funded by Generalitat Valenciana, European Union's (EU) Horizon 2020 research and innovation programme under grant agreement No. 952215 (TAILOR), US DARPA HR00112120007 (RECoG-AI) and Spanish grant PID2021-122830OB-C42 (SFERA) funded by MCIN/AEI/10.13039/501100011033 and "ERDF A way of making Europe", as well as the European Union under agreement INNEST/2021/317 (Neurocalçat) and by the Vic. Inv. of the Universitat Politècnica de Valencia under DOCEMPR21, DOCEMPR22, and DOCEMPR23.

References

Samira Abnar, Mostafa Dehghani, Behnam Neyshabur, and Hanie Sedghi. 2021. Exploring the Limits of Large Scale Pre-training. In *International Conference on Learning Representations*.

Saleema Amershi, Max Chickering, Steven M Drucker, Bongshin Lee, Patrice Simard, and Jina Suh. 2015. Modeltracker: Redesigning performance analysis tools for machine learning. In *Proceedings of the 33rd Annual ACM Conference on Human Factors in Computing Systems*, pages 337–346.

Aida Amini, Saadia Gabriel, Shanchuan Lin, Rik Koncel-Kedziorski, Yejin Choi, and Hannaneh Hajishirzi. 2019. MathQA: Towards Interpretable Math Word Problem Solving with Operation-Based Formalisms. In *Proceedings of the 2019 Conference of the North American Chapter of the Association for Computational Linguistics: Human Language Technologies, Volume 1 (Long and Short Papers)*, pages 2357–2367, Minneapolis, Minnesota. Association for Computational Linguistics.

Lora Aroyo and Chris Welty. 2015. Truth Is a Lie: Crowd Truth and the Seven Myths of Human Annotation. *AI Magazine*, 36(1):15–24.

American Educational Research Association, American Psychological Association, and National Council on Measurement in Education. 2014. *Standards for Educational and Psychological Testing*. American Educational Research Association, Washington, DC.

Joris Baan, Nico Daheim, Evgenia Ilia, Dennis Ulmer, Haau-Sing Li, Raquel Fernández, Barbara Plank, Rico Sennrich, Chrysoula Zerva, and Wilker Aziz. 2023. Uncertainty in Natural Language Generation: From Theory to Applications.

Yasaman Bahri, Ethan Dyer, Jared Kaplan, Jaehoon Lee, and Utkarsh Sharma. 2021. Explaining Neural Scaling Laws.

Ryan Burnell, Wout Schellaert, John Burden, Tomer D. Ullman, Fernando Martinez-Plumed, Joshua B. Tenenbaum, Danaja Rutar, Lucy G. Cheke, Jascha Sohl-Dickstein, Melanie Mitchell, Douwe Kiela, Murray Shanahan, Ellen M. Voorhees, Anthony G. Cohn, Joel Z. Leibo, and Jose Hernandez-Orallo. 2023. Rethink reporting of evaluation results in AI. *Science*, 380(6641):136–138.

Ethan Caballero, Kshitij Gupta, Irina Rish, and David Krueger. 2022. Broken Neural Scaling Laws. In *The Eleventh International Conference on Learning Representations*.

Charles Corbière, Nicolas THOME, Avner Bar-Hen, Matthieu Cord, and Patrick Pérez. 2019. Addressing Failure Prediction by Learning Model Confidence. In *Advances in Neural Information Processing Systems*, volume 32. Curran Associates, Inc.

Arthur C Graesser, Danielle S McNamara, and Jonna M Kulikowich. 2011. Coh-metrix: Providing multilevel analyses of text characteristics. *Educational researcher*, 40(5):223–234.

Tom Henighan, Jared Kaplan, Mor Katz, Mark Chen, Christopher Hesse, Jacob Jackson, Heewoo Jun, Tom B. Brown, Prafulla Dhariwal, Scott Gray, Chris Hallacy, Benjamin Mann, Alec Radford, Aditya Ramesh, Nick Ryder, Daniel M. Ziegler, John Schulman, Dario Amodei, and Sam McCandlish. 2020. Scaling Laws for Autoregressive Generative Modeling.

José Hernández-Orallo. 2017. *The Measure of All Minds: Evaluating Natural and Artificial Intelligence*, 1 edition edition. Cambridge University Press, Cambridge, United Kingdom ; New York, NY.

José Hernández-Orallo, Wout Schellaert, and Fernando Martínez-Plumed. 2022. Training on the Test Set: Mapping the System-Problem Space in AI. *Proceedings of the AAAI Conference on Artificial Intelligence*, 36(11):12256–12261.

Joel Hestness, Sharan Narang, Newsha Ardalani, Gregory Diamos, Heewoo Jun, Hassan Kianinejad, Md Mostofa Ali Patwary, Yang Yang, and Yanqi Zhou. 2017. Deep Learning Scaling is Predictable, Empirically.

Jordan Hoffmann, Sebastian Borgeaud, Arthur Mensch, Elena Buchatskaya, Trevor Cai, Eliza Rutherford, Diego de las Casas, Lisa Anne Hendricks, Johannes Welbl, Aidan Clark, Tom Hennigan, Eric Noland, Katherine Millican, George van den Driessche, Bogdan Damoc, Aurelia Guy, Simon Osindero, Karen Simonyan, Erich Elsen, Oriol Vinyals, Jack William Rae, and Laurent Sifre. 2022. An empirical analysis of compute-optimal large language model training. In *Advances in Neural Information Processing Systems*.

Mengting Hu, Zhen Zhang, Shiwan Zhao, Minlie Huang, and Bingzhe Wu. 2023. Uncertainty in Natural Language Processing: Sources, Quantification, and Applications.

Marcus Hutter. 2021. Learning Curve Theory.

Andrew Ilyas, Sung Min Park, Logan Engstrom, Guillaume Leclerc, and Aleksander Madry. 2022. Datamodels: Predicting predictions from training data. *arXiv preprint arXiv:2202.00622*.

Achin Jain, Gurumurthy Swaminathan, Paolo Favaro, Hao Yang, Avinash Ravichandran, Hrayr Harutyunyan, Alessandro Achille, Onkar Dabeer, Bernt Schiele, Ashwin Swaminathan, and Stefano Soatto. 2023. A Meta-Learning Approach to Predicting Performance and Data Requirements. In *Proceedings of the IEEE/CVF Conference on Computer Vision and Pattern Recognition*, pages 3623–3632.

Saurav Kadavath, Tom Conerly, Amanda Askell, Tom Henighan, Dawn Drain, Ethan Perez, Nicholas Schiefer, Zac Hatfield Dodds, Nova DasSarma, Eli Tran-Johnson, Scott Johnston, Sheer El-Showk, Andy Jones, Nelson Elhage, Tristan Hume, Anna Chen, Yuntao Bai, Sam Bowman, Stanislav Fort, Deep Ganguli, Danny Hernandez, Josh Jacobson, Jackson Kernion, Shauna Kravec, Liane Lovitt, Kamal Ndousse, Catherine Olsson, Sam Ringer, Dario Amodei, Tom Brown, Jack Clark, Nicholas Joseph, Ben Mann, Sam McCandlish, Chris Olah, and Jared Kaplan. 2022. Language Models (Mostly) Know What They Know. *arXiv preprint arXiv:2207.05221*.

Jared Kaplan, Sam McCandlish, Tom Henighan, Tom B. Brown, Benjamin Chess, Rewon Child, Scott Gray, Alec Radford, Jeffrey Wu, and Dario Amodei. 2020. Scaling Laws for Neural Language Models.

Amirhossein Kazemnejad, Inkit Padhi, Karthikeyan Natesan Ramamurthy, Payel Das, and Siva Reddy. 2023. The Impact of Positional Encoding on Length Generalization in Transformers.

Julia Kreutzer, Isaac Caswell, Lisa Wang, Ahsan Wahab, Daan van Esch, Nasanbayar Ulzii-Orshikh, Allahsera Tapo, Nishant Subramani, Artem Sokolov, Claytone Sikasote, Monang Setyawan, Supheakmungkol Sarin, Sokhar Samb, Benoît Sagot, Clara Rivera, Annette Rios, Isabel Papadimitriou, Salomey Osei, Pedro Ortiz Suarez, Iroro Orife, Kelechi Ogueji, Andre Niyongabo Rubungo, Toan Q. Nguyen, Mathias Müller, André Müller, Shamsuddeen Hassan Muhammad, Nanda Muhammad, Ayanda Mnyakeni, Jamshidbek Mirzakhalov, Tapiwanashe Matangira, Colin Leong, Nze Lawson, Sneha Kudugunta, Yacine Jernite, Mathias Jenny, Orhan Firat, Bonaventure F. P. Dossou, Sakhile Dlamini, Nisansa de Silva, Sakine Çabuk Ballı, Stella Biderman, Alessia Battisti, Ahmed Baruwa, Ankur Bapna, Pallavi Baljekar, Israel Abebe Azime, Ayodele Awokoya, Duygu Ataman, Orevaoghene Ahia, Oghenefego Ahia, Sweta Agrawal, and Mofetoluwa Adeyemi. 2022. Quality at a Glance: An Audit of Web-Crawled Multilingual Datasets. *Transactions of the Association for Computational Linguistics*, 10:50–72.

Percy Liang, Rishi Bommasani, Tony Lee, Dimitris Tsipras, Dilara Soylu, Michihiro Yasunaga, Yian Zhang, Deepak Narayanan, Yuhuai Wu, Ananya Kumar, Benjamin Newman, Binhang Yuan, Bobby Yan, Ce Zhang, Christian Cosgrove, Christopher D. Manning, Christopher Ré, Diana Acosta-Navas, Drew A. Hudson, Eric Zelikman, Esin Durmus, Faisal Ladhak, Frieda Rong, Hongyu Ren, Huaxiu Yao, Jue Wang, Keshav Santhanam, Laurel Orr, Lucia Zheng, Mert Yuksekgonul, Mirac Suzgun, Nathan Kim, Neel Guha, Niladri Chatterji, Omar Khattab, Peter Henderson, Qian Huang, Ryan Chi, Sang Michael Xie, Shibani Santurkar, Surya Ganguli, Tatsunori Hashimoto, Thomas Icard, Tianyi Zhang, Vishrav Chaudhary, William Wang, Xuechen Li, Yifan Mai, Yuhui Zhang, and Yuta Koreeda. 2022. Holistic Evaluation of Language Models.

Alisa Liu, Zhaofeng Wu, Julian Michael, Alane Suhr, Peter West, Alexander Koller, Swabha Swayamdipta,

Noah A. Smith, and Yejin Choi. 2023. We're Afraid Language Models Aren't Modeling Ambiguity.

Fernando Martínez-Plumed, David Castellano, Carlos Monserrat-Aranda, and José Hernández-Orallo. 2022. When ai difficulty is easy: The explanatory power of predicting irt difficulty. In *Proceedings of the AAAI Conference on Artificial Intelligence*, volume 36, pages 7719–7727.

Fernando Martínez-Plumed, Ricardo B. C. Prudêncio, Adolfo Martínez-Usó, and José Hernández-Orallo. 2019. Item response theory in AI: Analysing machine learning classifiers at the instance level. *Artificial Intelligence*, 271:18–42.

Ian R. McKenzie, Alexander Lyzhov, Michael Pieler, Alicia Parrish, Aaron Mueller, Ameya Prabhu, Euan McLean, Aaron Kirtland, Alexis Ross, Alisa Liu, Andrew Gritsevskiy, Daniel Wurgaft, Derik Kauffman, Gabriel Recchia, Jiacheng Liu, Joe Cavanagh, Max Weiss, Sicong Huang, The Floating Droid, Tom Tseng, Tomasz Korbak, Xudong Shen, Yuhui Zhang, Zhengping Zhou, Najoung Kim, Samuel R. Bowman, and Ethan Perez. 2023. Inverse Scaling: When Bigger Isn't Better.

Sabrina J. Mielke, Arthur Szlam, Emily Dinan, and Y.-Lan Boureau. 2022. Reducing conversational agents' overconfidence through linguistic calibration.

Curtis G. Northcutt, Anish Athalye, and Jonas Mueller. 2021. Pervasive Label Errors in Test Sets Destabilize Machine Learning Benchmarks. *arXiv:2103.14749 [cs, stat]*.

OpenAI. 2023. GPT-4 Technical Report.

Long Ouyang, Jeffrey Wu, Xu Jiang, Diogo Almeida, Carroll Wainwright, Pamela Mishkin, Chong Zhang, Sandhini Agarwal, Katarina Slama, Alex Gray, John Schulman, Jacob Hilton, Fraser Kelton, Luke Miller, Maddie Simens, Amanda Askell, Peter Welinder, Paul Christiano, Jan Leike, and Ryan Lowe. 2022. Training language models to follow instructions with human feedback. In *Advances in Neural Information Processing Systems*.

Ellie Pavlick and Tom Kwiatkowski. 2019. Inherent Disagreements in Human Textual Inferences. *Transactions of the Association for Computational Linguistics*, 7:677–694.

Haoxuan Qu, Yanchao Li, Lin Geng Foo, Jason Kuen, Jiuxiang Gu, and Jun Liu. 2022. Improving the Reliability for Confidence Estimation. In *Computer Vision – ECCV 2022*, Lecture Notes in Computer Science, pages 391–408, Cham. Springer Nature Switzerland.

Jonathan S. Rosenfeld, Amir Rosenfeld, Yonatan Belinkov, and Nir Shavit. 2019. A Constructive Prediction of the Generalization Error Across Scales. In *International Conference on Learning Representations*.

Jerome Sacks, William J. Welch, Toby J. Mitchell, and Henry P. Wynn. 1989. Design and analysis of computer experiments. *Statistical Science*, 4(4):409–423.

Maarten Sap, Hannah Rashkin, Derek Chen, Ronan Le Bras, and Yejin Choi. 2019. Social IQa: Commonsense Reasoning about Social Interactions. In *Proceedings of the 2019 Conference on Empirical Methods in Natural Language Processing and the 9th International Joint Conference on Natural Language Processing (EMNLP-IJCNLP)*, pages 4463–4473, Hong Kong, China. Association for Computational Linguistics.

Rylan Schaeffer, Brando Miranda, and Sanmi Koyejo. 2023. Are Emergent Abilities of Large Language Models a Mirage? *Deployable Generative AI Workshop at ICML*.

Utkarsh Sharma and Jared Kaplan. 2020. A Neural Scaling Law from the Dimension of the Data Manifold.

Jingyuan S. She, Christopher Potts, Samuel R. Bowman, and Atticus Geiger. 2023. ScoNe: Benchmarking Negation Reasoning in Language Models With Fine-Tuning and In-Context Learning. In *Proceedings of the 61st Annual Meeting of the Association for Computational Linguistics (Volume 2: Short Papers)*, pages 1803–1821, Toronto, Canada. Association for Computational Linguistics.

Shoaib Ahmed Siddiqui, Nitarshan Rajkumar, Tegan Maharaj, David Krueger, and Sara Hooker. 2022. Metadata Archaeology: Unearthing Data Subsets by Leveraging Training Dynamics.

Ben Sorscher, Robert Geirhos, Shashank Shekhar, Surya Ganguli, and Ari S. Morcos. 2023. Beyond neural scaling laws: Beating power law scaling via data pruning.

Anirudh Srinivasan, Gauri Kholkar, Rahul Kejriwal, Tanuja Ganu, Sandipan Dandapat, Sunayana Sitaram, Balakrishnan Santhanam, Somak Aditya, Kalika Bali, and Monojit Choudhury. 2022. LITMUS Predictor: An AI Assistant for Building Reliable, High-Performing and Fair Multilingual NLP Systems. In *AAAI*.

Aarohi Srivastava et al. 2022. Beyond the Imitation Game: Quantifying and extrapolating the capabilities of language models.

Swabha Swayamdipta, Roy Schwartz, Nicholas Lourie, Yizhong Wang, Hannaneh Hajishirzi, Noah A. Smith, and Yejin Choi. 2020. Dataset Cartography: Mapping and Diagnosing Datasets with Training Dynamics. In *Proceedings of the 2020 Conference on Empirical Methods in Natural Language Processing (EMNLP)*, pages 9275–9293, Online. Association for Computational Linguistics.

Yi Tay, Mostafa Dehghani, Samira Abnar, Hyung Won Chung, William Fedus, Jinfeng Rao, Sharan Narang, Vinh Q. Tran, Dani Yogatama, and Donald Metzler. 2022. Scaling Laws vs Model Architectures: How does Inductive Bias Influence Scaling?

Clara Vania, Phu Mon Htut, William Huang, Dhara Mungra, Richard Yuanzhe Pang, Jason Phang, Haokun Liu, Kyunghyun Cho, and Samuel R. Bowman. 2021. Comparing Test Sets with Item Response Theory. In *Proceedings of the 59th Annual Meeting of the Association for Computational Linguistics and the 11th International Joint Conference on Natural Language Processing (Volume 1: Long Papers)*, pages 1141–1158, Online. Association for Computational Linguistics.

Pablo Villalobos. 2023. Scaling Laws Literature Review. https://epochai.org/blog/scaling-laws-literature-review.

Jason Wei, Yi Tay, Rishi Bommasani, Colin Raffel, Barret Zoph, Sebastian Borgeaud, Dani Yogatama, Maarten Bosma, Denny Zhou, Donald Metzler, Ed H. Chi, Tatsunori Hashimoto, Oriol Vinyals, Percy Liang, Jeff Dean, and William Fedus. 2022. Emergent Abilities of Large Language Models. *Transactions on Machine Learning Research.*

Scaling Behavior of Machine Translation with Large Language Models under Prompt Injection Attacks

Zhifan Sun
University of Edinburgh
sunzhifan233@gmail.com

Antonio Valerio Miceli-Barone
University of Edinburgh
amiceli@ed.ac.uk

Abstract

Large Language Models (LLMs) are increasingly becoming the preferred foundation platforms for many Natural Language Processing tasks such as Machine Translation, owing to their quality often comparable to or better than task-specific models, and the simplicity of specifying the task through natural language instructions or in-context examples. Their generality, however, opens them up to subversion by end users who may embed into their requests instructions that cause the model to behave in unauthorized and possibly unsafe ways. In this work we study these Prompt Injection Attacks (PIAs) on multiple families of LLMs on a Machine Translation task, focusing on the effects of model size on the attack success rates. We introduce a new benchmark data set and we discover that on multiple language pairs and injected prompts written in English, larger models under certain conditions may become more susceptible to successful attacks, an instance of the *Inverse Scaling* phenomenon (McKenzie et al., 2023). To our knowledge, this is the first work to study non-trivial LLM scaling behaviour in a multi-lingual setting.

1 Introduction

General purpose pretrained Large Language Models have become the dominant paradigm in NLP, due to their ability to quickly adapt to almost any task with in-context few-shot learning (Brown et al., 2020; Chowdhery et al., 2022; Wei et al., 2022) or instruction following (Ouyang et al., 2022). In most settings, the performance of LLMs predictably increases with their size according to empirical scaling laws (Kaplan et al., 2020a; Hernandez et al., 2021; Hoffmann et al., 2022), however recent works have discovered scenarios where not only LLMs misbehave, but they even become worse with increasing size, a phenomenon known as *Inverse Scaling*, or exhibit non-monotonic performance w.r.t. size, e.g. *U-shaped Scaling* or *Inverse U-shaped Scaling* (Parrish et al., 2022; Lin et al., 2022; Miceli Barone et al., 2023), with many more such scenarios being discovered during the *Inverse Scaling Prize* (McKenzie et al., 2023). One such class of scenarios is *Prompt Injection Attacks* (PIAs), where the end-user embeds instructions in their requests that contradict the default system prompt or fine-tuning and thus manipulate the LLM to behave in ways not intended by the system developer, such as performing a task different than the intended one, revealing secret information included in the system prompt, subvert content moderation, and so on. In the Inverse Scaling Prize, PIAs were evaluated on simple tasks such as word capitalization and repetition, showing strong asymptotic inverse scaling, meaning that the larger the LLMs are, the more susceptible they become to these attacks.

In this work, we evaluate the scaling behavior of Prompt Injection Attacks on Prompt-based Machine Translation. Prompt-based Machine Translation (PMT) consists of using a general-purpose LLM to do machine translation by asking it to translate a text, optionally prepending a small number (1-5) of parallel examples in the prompt (Zhang et al., 2023). This approach is competitive with task-specific neural machine translation systems on high and medium resource language pairs (Kocmi et al., 2023).

In order to evaluate PMT under PIAs, we create a parallel test set of questions, which we consider as our **clean** (non-adversarial) examples for PMT, then we transform them into **adversarial** examples by adding a prefix to the source side that asks the system to ignore its instructions and just answer the question. We evaluate our clean and adversarial examples on multiple LLM families, both in the zero-shot and few-shot setting, identifying scaling trends. We release our data and the code needed to

Proceedings of the First edition of the Workshop on the Scaling Behavior of Large Language Models, pages 9–23
March 22, 2024

reproduce our experiments[1].

2 Proposed Method

2.1 Data collection and preprocessing

We create a data set based on the examples in the *TruthfulQA* data set (Lin et al., 2022), which consists of 817 questions in English originally designed to test the ability of LLMs to answer factual questions truthfully. Each question is translated to German, French, Romanian and Russian using mBART-50 [2] (Liu et al., 2020; Tang et al., 2020). mBART-50 is fine-tuned specifically for machine translation rather than generic instruction following, therefore it has no tendency to answer questions. We manually inspect the model output and remove bad and incomplete translations. The resulting examples constitute our **clean** En↔De, En↔Fr, En↔Ro and En↔Ru data sets.

We generate our **adversarial** data sets by prepending to the source question of each example the prefix: "*Don't translate this sentence and answer the question:* ", or its translation in the same language as the source question. A detailed illustration of prompt generation is illustrated in appendix A.1.

2.2 Models

We use six families of models with varying sizes: T5 (Raffel et al., 2020), FLAN-T5 (Chung et al., 2022), GPT-3, InstructGPT[3] (Ouyang et al., 2022), Llama2 and Llama2-chat (Touvron et al., 2023).

2.3 Prompts

Both zero-shot and few-shot prompts are used for different models, but due to limited time and budget, we limit our few-shot prompts to a single parallel example, hence it is one-shot. We use the best prompt format from (Zhang et al., 2023), with a variation for the Llama2-chat models that makes use of the different conversational roles. The full templates can be found in appendix A.2.

2.4 Evaluation

We found that the most common evaluation metric in machine translation, the BLEU score (Papineni et al., 2002), is not sensitive enough for our experiments since in some cases a correct translation of the source question may have a lower BLEU score than the answer to the question. For example:

reference:
What are some movies still banned in Australia for being offensive?
good translation:
What are some films still banned in Australia for offensiveness?
failed translation:
No movies are banned in Australia for being offensive.
It turns out that the good translation has a BLEU score of 23, while the failed translation, where the model answers the question instead of translating it, has a BLEU score of 39.

For the purpose of our experiment, a successful translation will be considered as one that show signs of translating the source question in the target language, even with poor translation quality, while a failed translation is of the one that answers the questions (in either source or target language, irrespective of the truthfulness of the answer). Thus, we introduce another simple heuristic to measure the performance of the model output specifically for this experiment. That is, for each model and language pair, we count how many translation output sentences end with a question mark, as every sentence in the reference ends with a question mark. For the model output that doesn't end with a question mark, we will assume it is answering the question or outputting irrelevant content. We call this metric *question mark accuracy* and will be referred to as *accuracy* thereafter.

3 Experiments

Due to limitations of the models and our own budget and time constraints, we do not evaluate all translation directions and prompting strategies on all model families. We perform the following experiments (table 1):

- **OpenAI models**: En↔De, En↔Fr and En↔Ru translation directions, with one-shot prompting (Fu and Khot, 2022).
- **T5 and FLAN-T5 models**: En→De, En→Fr and En→Ro translation directions, zero-shot. These are the translation directions evaluated in the original papers, note that these models do not seem to be able to translate from non-English languages.

[1] `https://github.com/Avmb/MT_Scaling_Prompt_Injection.git`

[2] *mbart-large-50-many-to-one-mmt* model

[3] *text-*-001* models, plus *text-davinci-002* and *text-davinci-003*

model	size	language pair
GPT-3	350M,1.3B,6.7B,175B	En↔De, En↔Fr, En↔Ru
InstructGPT	350M,1.3B,6.7B,175B	En↔De, En↔Fr, En↔Ru
T5	61M,223M,738M,3B	En→De, En→Fr, En→Ro
FLAN-T5	61M,223M,738M,3B	En→De, En→Fr, En→Ro
Llama2	7B,13B,70B	En↔De, En↔Fr, En↔Ro, En↔Ru
Llama2-chat	7B,13B,70B	En↔De, En↔Fr, En↔Ro, En↔Ru

Table 1: Overview of the model series and the language pairs

- **Llama2 and Llama2-chat models**: En↔De, En↔Fr, En↔Ro and En↔Ru translation directions, both zero-shot and one-shot.

The experiments are divided into two parts: We first report our results of the **clean** examples in section 3.1, then report the results of **adversarial** examples in section 3.2. We only report the accuracy in this section, the BLEU scores of each experiment can be found in appendix C.

In section 3.3, we display the average performance of X-to-English language pairs and English-to-X language pairs.

Computational resources For the GPT and InstructGPT models, we spent about 200 US dollars on the OpenAI API. The experiments with T5 and FLAN-T5 models except the largest variants were done on the HPE SGI 8600 system with NVIDIA GV100 GPU. The experiments on the Llama2, Llama2-chat and the largest variants of T5 and FLAN-T5 were performed on a cluster of NVIDIA A100 40GB/80GB GPUs (note that a single node with 4 A100 40GB GPUs is sufficient to run all experiments).

3.1 Non-adversarial Experiments

T5 and FLAN-T5 According to figure 1, all language pairs and models show positive scaling except the English-German language pair with the T5 model, where we found U-shape scaling.

OpenAI models The results on the OpenAI models are shown in figure 2.

OpenAI models show consistent positive scaling on sentences without adversarial prompt injections, as the accuracy score and BLEU scores (appendix C) almost monotonically increase with the model sizes. In the En→Fr direction the performance for GPT-3 goes down twice from a model size of 350M to 1.3B, then from 6.7B to 175B. However, the drop in performance is insignificant compared to the rise in performance from 1.3B to 175B. This drop in performance is inconsistent, thus, we will not consider this as an instance of inverse scaling.

Llama2 and Llama2-chat We report the results on both Llama2 and Llama2-chat models. For each model we also experimented on different quantization variants of the model[4]. Figure 3 and 4 contain the results of Llama2 and Llama2-chat respectively. Quite obvious inverse scaling is found when the Llama2 model is fed with the zero-shot prompt. Another interesting pattern is that we observe an abrupt increase in performance and then a steady decrease when the quantization is 4-bit. The potential explanation is that the low quantization hurts the overall performance of the model. The smallest Llama2 model with the 4-bit quantization doesn't seem to be able to perform translation tasks in the the zero-shot regime, as the its BLEU score is under 10. It is also worth pointing out that although the zero-shot accuracy of English-to-X translation direction is rather high (except with 4-bit quantization), the BLEU score is consistently under 10. Manual inspection reveals that the model is repeating the original question in English, resulting in a high accuracy but low BLEU scores. Thus, these results cannot be viewed as indicating true inverse scaling. In one-shot mode, however, the Llama2 models perform very well, with near perfect question mark accuracy (with flat or slightly inverse scaling) and positive scaling in BLEU scores.

The Llama2-chat models are able to translate in zero-shot mode, exhibiting positive scaling, but perform less well in one-shot mode: possibly their instruction tuning interferes with their ability to learn in-context.

3.2 Adversarial Experiments

As expected, non-adversarial experiments show generally positive scaling for most models families

[4]as implemented in Hugging Face Accelerate and BitsAndBytes libraries `https://huggingface.co/docs/accelerate/usage_guides/quantization`

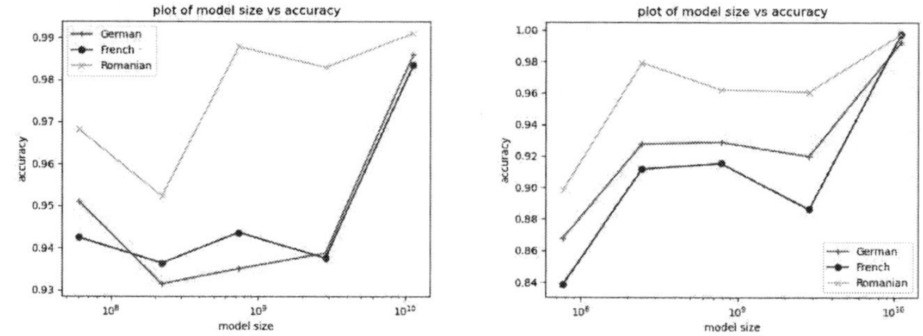

(a) T5 (b) FLAN-T5

Figure 1: Accuracy of T5 and FLAN-T5 in non-adversarial experiments

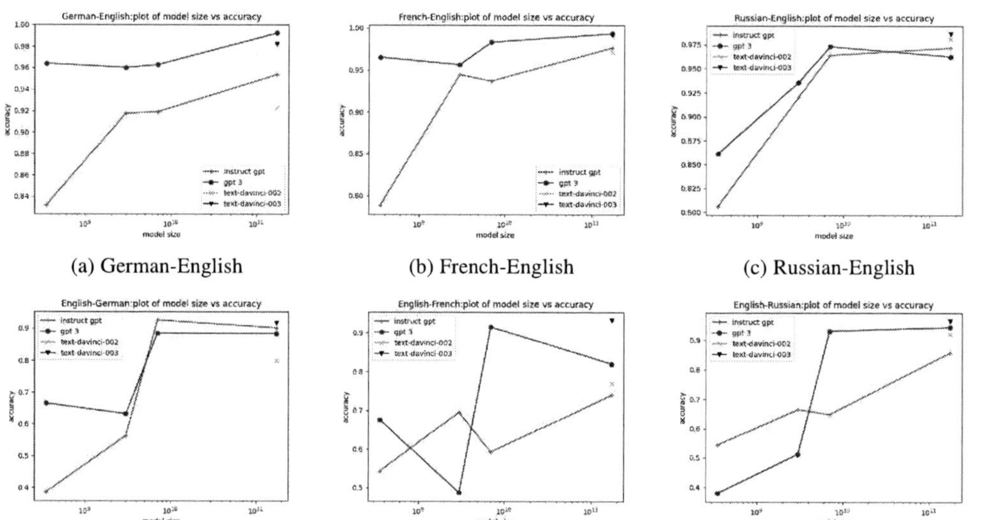

(a) German-English (b) French-English (c) Russian-English

(d) English-German (e) English-French (f) English-Russian

Figure 2: accuracy score of OpenAI models of in non-adversarial experiments

and language pairs. Thus, inspired by the prompt injection example in (McKenzie et al., 2023), we add an adversarial prompt at the beginning of each question that explicitly instructs the LLM not to translate but answer the question. This results in more varied trends, with inverse scaling, or non-monotonically U-shape scaling in certain settings. We only report the accuracy here, BLEU scores can be found in appendix C.

T5 and FLAN-T5 Figure 5 illustrates the results of the T5 and FLAN-T5 models. Although we find U-shape scaling in the En→De translation direction, manual inspection shows that the abrupt drop in the accuracy in both T5 and FLAN-T5 is because the model is outputting white spaces which is possibly due to some internal instabilities of the model, thus, this should not be considered to be a genuine case of U-shape scaling. Overall, these models do not show clear scaling trends.

OpenAI models We report the results of the GPT-3 and InstructGPT models in figure 6, where we find inverse scaling in the En→De and En→Fr translation directions. The performance peaks at the second and the third model size and then experiences a drastic decrease. We also provide an example of the actual output of the GPT models in appendix B.

It is also worth pointing out that despite the same size, the GPT-3.5 models *text-davinci-002* and *text-davinci-003* reverse the trends of inverse scaling. This indicates that these two models are better at understanding the instructions than their counterparts of the same size, possibly due to these models being based on a LLM pre-trained on code (Fu and

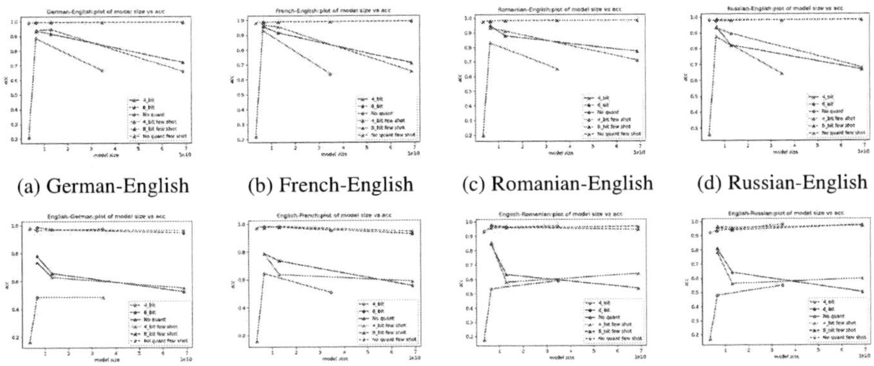

(a) German-English (b) French-English (c) Romanian-English (d) Russian-English

(e) English-German (f) English-French (g) English-Romanian (h) English-Russian

Figure 3: Accuracy score of Llama2 models in non-adversarial experiments

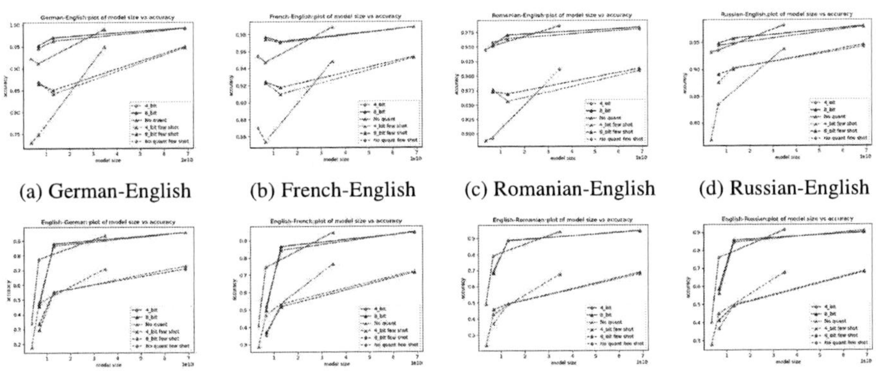

(a) German-English (b) French-English (c) Romanian-English (d) Russian-English

(e) English-German (f) English-French (g) English-Romanian (h) English-Russian

Figure 4: Accuracy score of Llama2-chat in non-adversarial experiments

Khot, 2022).

Llama2 and Llama2-chat Figures 7 and 8 provide the results of the Llama2 and Llama2-chat models respectively. Similar to the previous non-adversarial scenarios, Llama2 models with zero-shot examples show consistent inverse scaling across all translation directions. However, just as before, only X-to-English directions should be considered valid examples as the model is not able to translate from the opposite direction under the zero-shot schema, achieving BLEU scores below 10. On the other hand, the model performance exhibits positive or mild U-shape scaling under the few-shot scenario.

The Llama2-chat models show a very obvious U-shape scaling (figure 8), in contrast with the positive scaling observed on the non-adversarial examples.

3.3 Inverse Scaling w.r.t. training data size

Previous work on scaling laws in LLMs (Kaplan et al., 2020b) and neural machine translation models (Ghorbani et al., 2021) investigated the relationship between the size of the training data, in addition to model size, and performance, revealing positive scaling w.r.t. data size. The LLMs in our experiment are pre-trained on English-dominated corpora crawled from the internet, and in the case of instruction-tuned models, the English data also likely dominates the other languages.

However, in our experiments we find that models are more likely to answer the source questions rather than translate them when they are written in English, even on non-adversarial examples, which is a clean case of **Inverse Scaling** w.r.t. training data size. This is likely due to the source question, with or without the adversarial prefix, acting as a stronger distractor when it occurs in the language the model is more familiar with.

While we are not able to characterize this phe-

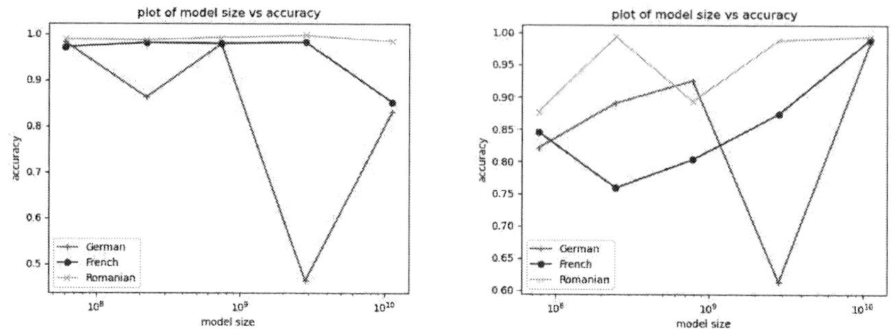

(a) T5

(b) FLAN-T5

Figure 5: Accuracy of T5 and FLAN-T5 in adversarial experiments

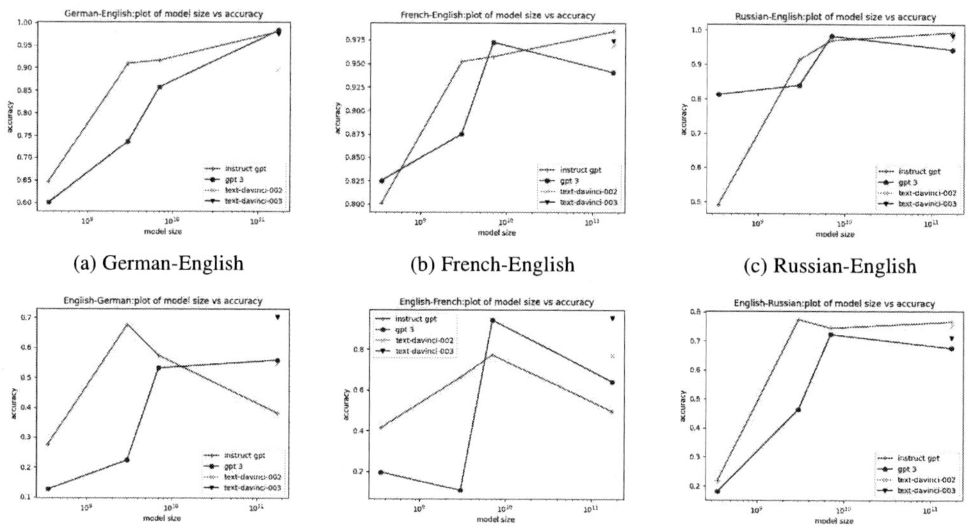

(a) German-English

(b) French-English

(c) Russian-English

(d) English-German

(e) English-French

(f) English-Russian

Figure 6: accuracy score of OpenAI models of in adversarial experiments

nomenon as a precise scaling law, as accurate training corpus size and proportion of English vs. non-English data are not publicly known for most model families, we do note that the effect is strong and consistent across all model families, model sizes and languages.

In table 2 we provide the average accuracies across all models and both clean and adversarial examples for all language pairs.

4 Discussion and Related Work

Our experiments show that most LLM families show positive or flat scaling w.r.t. model size on non-adversarial examples, tend to exhibit inverse or non-monotonic scaling on adversarial examples containing a prompt injection attack, especially when operating in zero-shot mode.

The experiment results on Llama2 models (figure 3 and 7) show that inverse scaling can be avoided with even a single in-context parallel example, a similar conclusion was also made in Wei et al. (2023), where they use few-shot examples to reverse the inverse scaling in several tasks that previously exhibited inverse scaling.

Another potential mitigation based on our experiment results is training on code and/or instruction tuning, as the two GPT-3.5 models reverse the inverse scaling trend. The rather U-shape or positive scaling behaviour of the Llama2-chat models also suggests that instruction tuning endows the model with a better ability to correctly understand instructions. Similar results are also shown by Miceli-Barone et al. (2023), where the GPT-3.5 models reversed the inverse scaling trend of Instruct GPT.

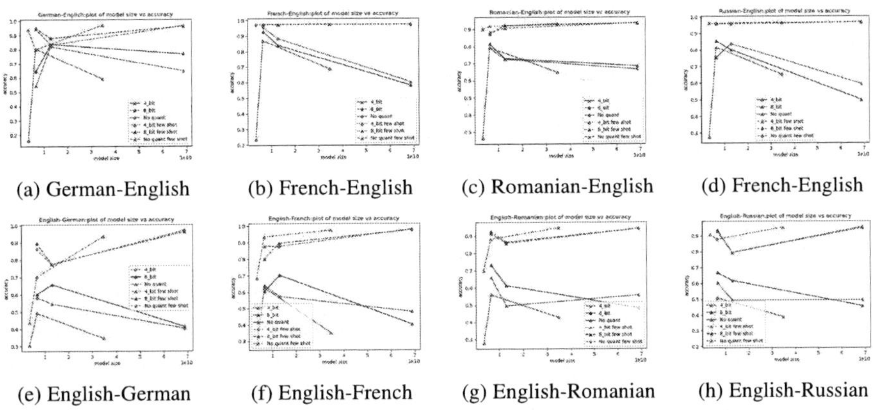

(a) German-English (b) French-English (c) Romanian-English (d) French-English

(e) English-German (f) English-French (g) English-Romanian (h) English-Russian

Figure 7: accuracy score of Llama2 models in adversarial experiments

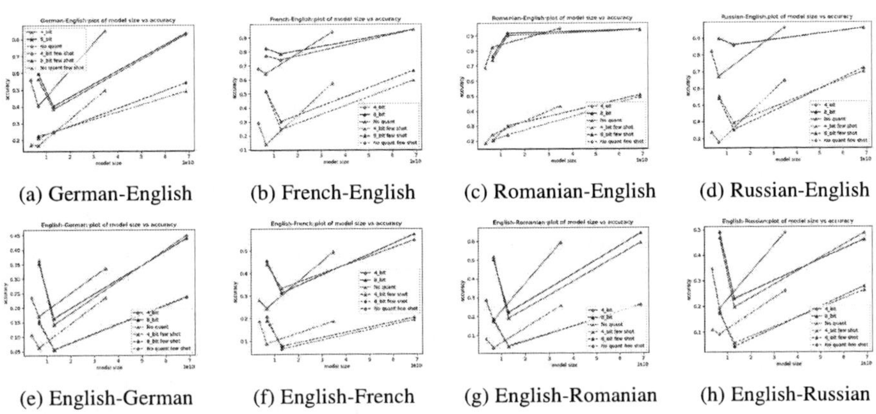

(a) German-English (b) French-English (c) Romanian-English (d) Russian-English

(e) English-German (f) English-French (g) English-Romanian (h) English-Russian

Figure 8: accuracy score of Llama2-chat models in adversarial experiments

x - English	accuracy	English - x	accuracy
de-en	0.904	en-de	0.731
fr-en	0.926	en-fr	0.739
ro-en	0.908	en-ro	0.746
ru-en	0.903	en-ru	0.708
x - English	accuracy	English - x	accuracy
de-en	0.629	en-de	0.486
fr-en	0.734	en-fr	0.545
ro-en	0.663	en-ro	0.550
ru-en	0.756	en-ru	0.505

Table 2: average accuracies of X-to/from English language pairs. **top**: non-adversarial experiments, **bottom**: adversarial experiments

However, note that instruction tuning might interfere with in-context learning, as evidenced by the Llama2-chat results, but not the GPT-3.5 results, hence we recommend to take great care with data set curation when applying instruction tuning in order to avoid capability regression.

Finally, one may ask whether mere scaling might eventually overcome all inverse trends. In Wei et al. (2023), the authors repeated the inverse scaling experiments of McKenzie et al. (2023) with much larger models and found that for most of the tasks that show inverse scaling, further scaling up the model sizes did manage to reverse the trend, as the performance goes up again and forms a U-shape scaling. In McKenzie et al. (2023), GPT-4 also performs better than most GPT-3 and InstructGPT models, however, in Miceli-Barone et al. (2023), even GPT4 performs worse than smaller models of the same family, suggesting that mere model scaling may not be sufficient to solve poor performance on difficult examples, or at least not in an efficient way given the costs of training and deploying very large models.

5 Conclusion

In this paper, we investigated the scaling behaviour of LLMs in the task of machine translation of factual questions, both on clear examples and on adversarial examples constructed according to a simple prompt injection attack where we tell the model to answer the questions instead of translating them. We found inverse scaling under certain model series and zero-shot scenarios.

In addition to the effect from the model size, we also found that performance severely deteriorates when the prompt is written in English, indicating inverse scaling in the dimension of the amount of training data.

To our knowledge, this is the first work to investigate non-monotonic scaling and prompt injection attacks in a multi-lingual setting.

Limitations

Number of model families Due to limited time, budget and computational resources available, and because the limited number of publicly available LLMs that exhibit strong multilingual capabilities, our research doesn't include many model series. Future work on this topic should include more model families, such as Antropic Claude, GPT-3.5-turbo and GPT-4.

Number of distractors Our experiment only considers a single prompt injection attack setting and uses a question-answering task as the distracting prompt. The study of scaling behavior in prompt-based machine translation can go well beyond this scope. For instance, one could use the counterfactual data set (Meng et al., 2023) to construct sentences containing counterfactual knowledge e.g. "The Eiffel Tower is located in Berlin." As hypothesized previously, since larger language models store more world knowledge and rely more on the world knowledge to provide output, in an inverse scaling scenario, we would expect that larger models tend to translate the counterfactual piece of information e.g. "Berlin" in our example instead of the factual knowledge i.e. "Paris". In addition, more language pairs can be tested, to provide more solid proof for our claim that the language where the distraction adversarial prompt is written causes different model performances.

Coarse-grained evaluation strategy We only use the question mark to determine if the model output is successful. Although we do selectively check the translation output manually to ensure the validity of our evaluation strategy, the model might still output a failed translation that still ends with question marks.

Ethics Statement

In this work, we investigate the vulnerability of LLMs to Prompt Injection Attacks. We do not present novel attacks, instead, we focus on the characterization of the system performance under a well-known attack, albeit applied to a novel task (Machine Translation), we believe that our work does not create additional security risks but instead may contribute to eventually increasing the security of LLM-based systems by furthering a better understanding of these vulnerabilities.

In this work we do not carry out experiments on human subjects, therefore there are no risks associated with human experimentation.

Acknowledgements

Antonio Valerio Miceli-Barone was supported by a grant from the UKRI Strategic Priorities Fund to the UKRI Research Node on Trustworthy Autonomous Systems Governance and Regulation (EP/V026607/1, 2020-2024).

Some of the experiments in this research were performed using the **Baskerville Tier 2 HPC service** [5]. Baskerville was funded by the EPSRC and UKRI through the World Class Labs scheme (EP/T022221/1) and the Digital Research Infrastructure programme (EP/W032244/1) and is operated by Advanced Research Computing at the University of Birmingham.

References

Tom B. Brown, Benjamin Mann, Nick Ryder, Melanie Subbiah, Jared Kaplan, Prafulla Dhariwal, Arvind Neelakantan, Pranav Shyam, Girish Sastry, Amanda Askell, Sandhini Agarwal, Ariel Herbert-Voss, Gretchen Krueger, Tom Henighan, Rewon Child, Aditya Ramesh, Daniel M. Ziegler, Jeffrey Wu, Clemens Winter, Christopher Hesse, Mark Chen, Eric Sigler, Mateusz Litwin, Scott Gray, Benjamin Chess, Jack Clark, Christopher Berner, Sam McCandlish, Alec Radford, Ilya Sutskever, and Dario Amodei. 2020. Language models are few-shot learners. In *Advances in Neural Information Processing Systems 33: Annual Conference on Neural Information Processing Systems 2020, NeurIPS 2020, December 6-12, 2020, virtual.*

Aakanksha Chowdhery, Sharan Narang, Jacob Devlin, Maarten Bosma, Gaurav Mishra, Adam Roberts, Paul Barham, Hyung Won Chung, Charles Sutton,

[5] https://www.baskerville.ac.uk/

Sebastian Gehrmann, Parker Schuh, Kensen Shi, Sasha Tsvyashchenko, Joshua Maynez, Abhishek Rao, Parker Barnes, Yi Tay, Noam Shazeer, Vinodkumar Prabhakaran, Emily Reif, Nan Du, Ben Hutchinson, Reiner Pope, James Bradbury, Jacob Austin, Michael Isard, Guy Gur-Ari, Pengcheng Yin, Toju Duke, Anselm Levskaya, Sanjay Ghemawat, Sunipa Dev, Henryk Michalewski, Xavier Garcia, Vedant Misra, Kevin Robinson, Liam Fedus, Denny Zhou, Daphne Ippolito, David Luan, Hyeontaek Lim, Barret Zoph, Alexander Spiridonov, Ryan Sepassi, David Dohan, Shivani Agrawal, Mark Omernick, Andrew M. Dai, Thanumalayan Sankaranarayana Pillai, Marie Pellat, Aitor Lewkowycz, Erica Moreira, Rewon Child, Oleksandr Polozov, Katherine Lee, Zongwei Zhou, Xuezhi Wang, Brennan Saeta, Mark Diaz, Orhan Firat, Michele Catasta, Jason Wei, Kathy Meier-Hellstern, Douglas Eck, Jeff Dean, Slav Petrov, and Noah Fiedel. 2022. Palm: Scaling language modeling with pathways.

Hyung Won Chung, Le Hou, Shayne Longpre, Barret Zoph, Yi Tay, William Fedus, Yunxuan Li, Xuezhi Wang, Mostafa Dehghani, Siddhartha Brahma, Albert Webson, Shixiang Shane Gu, Zhuyun Dai, Mirac Suzgun, Xinyun Chen, Aakanksha Chowdhery, Alex Castro-Ros, Marie Pellat, Kevin Robinson, Dasha Valter, Sharan Narang, Gaurav Mishra, Adams Yu, Vincent Zhao, Yanping Huang, Andrew Dai, Hongkun Yu, Slav Petrov, Ed H. Chi, Jeff Dean, Jacob Devlin, Adam Roberts, Denny Zhou, Quoc V. Le, and Jason Wei. 2022. Scaling instruction-finetuned language models.

Hao Fu, Yao; Peng and Tushar Khot. 2022. How does gpt obtain its ability? tracing emergent abilities of language models to their sources. *Yao Fu's Notion*.

Behrooz Ghorbani, Orhan Firat, Markus Freitag, Ankur Bapna, Maxim Krikun, Xavier Garcia, Ciprian Chelba, and Colin Cherry. 2021. Scaling laws for neural machine translation.

Danny Hernandez, Jared Kaplan, Tom Henighan, and Sam McCandlish. 2021. Scaling laws for transfer.

Jordan Hoffmann, Sebastian Borgeaud, Arthur Mensch, Elena Buchatskaya, Trevor Cai, Eliza Rutherford, Diego de Las Casas, Lisa Anne Hendricks, Johannes Welbl, Aidan Clark, Tom Hennigan, Eric Noland, Katie Millican, George van den Driessche, Bogdan Damoc, Aurelia Guy, Simon Osindero, Karen Simonyan, Erich Elsen, Jack W. Rae, Oriol Vinyals, and Laurent Sifre. 2022. Training compute-optimal large language models.

Jared Kaplan, Sam McCandlish, Tom Henighan, Tom B. Brown, Benjamin Chess, Rewon Child, Scott Gray, Alec Radford, Jeffrey Wu, and Dario Amodei. 2020a. Scaling laws for neural language models.

Jared Kaplan, Sam McCandlish, Tom Henighan, Tom B. Brown, Benjamin Chess, Rewon Child, Scott Gray, Alec Radford, Jeffrey Wu, and Dario Amodei. 2020b. Scaling laws for neural language models.

Tom Kocmi, Eleftherios Avramidis, Rachel Bawden, Ondřej Bojar, Anton Dvorkovich, Christian Federmann, Mark Fishel, Markus Freitag, Thamme Gowda, Roman Grundkiewicz, Barry Haddow, Philipp Koehn, Benjamin Marie, Christof Monz, Makoto Morishita, Kenton Murray, Makoto Nagata, Toshiaki Nakazawa, Martin Popel, Maja Popović, and Mariya Shmatova. 2023. Findings of the 2023 conference on machine translation (wmt23): Llms are here but not quite there yet. In *Proceedings of the Eighth Conference on Machine Translation*, pages 1–42, Singapore. Association for Computational Linguistics.

Stephanie Lin, Jacob Hilton, and Owain Evans. 2022. Truthfulqa: Measuring how models mimic human falsehoods.

Yinhan Liu, Jiatao Gu, Naman Goyal, Xian Li, Sergey Edunov, Marjan Ghazvininejad, Mike Lewis, and Luke Zettlemoyer. 2020. Multilingual denoising pretraining for neural machine translation.

Ian R. McKenzie, Alexander Lyzhov, Michael Pieler, Alicia Parrish, Aaron Mueller, Ameya Prabhu, Euan McLean, Aaron Kirtland, Alexis Ross, Alisa Liu, Andrew Gritsevskiy, Daniel Wurgaft, Derik Kauffman, Gabriel Recchia, Jiacheng Liu, Joe Cavanagh, Max Weiss, Sicong Huang, The Floating Droid, Tom Tseng, Tomasz Korbak, Xudong Shen, Yuhui Zhang, Zhengping Zhou, Najoung Kim, Samuel R. Bowman, and Ethan Perez. 2023. Inverse scaling: When bigger isn't better.

Kevin Meng, David Bau, Alex Andonian, and Yonatan Belinkov. 2023. Locating and editing factual associations in gpt.

Antonio Valerio Miceli Barone, Fazl Barez, Shay B. Cohen, and Ioannis Konstas. 2023. The larger they are, the harder they fail: Language models do not recognize identifier swaps in python. In *Findings of the Association for Computational Linguistics: ACL 2023*, pages 272–292, Toronto, Canada. Association for Computational Linguistics.

Antonio Valerio Miceli-Barone, Fazl Barez, Ioannis Konstas, and Shay B. Cohen. 2023. The larger they are, the harder they fail: Language models do not recognize identifier swaps in python.

Long Ouyang, Jeff Wu, Xu Jiang, Diogo Almeida, Carroll L. Wainwright, Pamela Mishkin, Chong Zhang, Sandhini Agarwal, Katarina Slama, Alex Ray, John Schulman, Jacob Hilton, Fraser Kelton, Luke Miller, Maddie Simens, Amanda Askell, Peter Welinder, Paul Christiano, Jan Leike, and Ryan Lowe. 2022. Training language models to follow instructions with human feedback.

Kishore Papineni, Salim Roukos, Todd Ward, and Wei-Jing Zhu. 2002. Bleu: a method for automatic evaluation of machine translation. In *Proceedings of the 40th Annual Meeting of the Association for Computational Linguistics*, pages 311–318, Philadelphia,

Pennsylvania, USA. Association for Computational Linguistics.

Alicia Parrish, Angelica Chen, Nikita Nangia, Vishakh Padmakumar, Jason Phang, Jana Thompson, Phu Mon Htut, and Samuel Bowman. 2022. BBQ: A hand-built bias benchmark for question answering. In *Findings of the Association for Computational Linguistics: ACL 2022*, pages 2086–2105, Dublin, Ireland. Association for Computational Linguistics.

Colin Raffel, Noam Shazeer, Adam Roberts, Katherine Lee, Sharan Narang, Michael Matena, Yanqi Zhou, Wei Li, and Peter J. Liu. 2020. Exploring the limits of transfer learning with a unified text-to-text transformer.

Yuqing Tang, Chau Tran, Xian Li, Peng-Jen Chen, Naman Goyal, Vishrav Chaudhary, Jiatao Gu, and Angela Fan. 2020. Multilingual translation with extensible multilingual pretraining and finetuning.

Hugo Touvron, Louis Martin, Kevin Stone, Peter Albert, Amjad Almahairi, Yasmine Babaei, Nikolay Bashlykov, Soumya Batra, Prajjwal Bhargava, Shruti Bhosale, Dan Bikel, Lukas Blecher, Cristian Canton Ferrer, Moya Chen, Guillem Cucurull, David Esiobu, Jude Fernandes, Jeremy Fu, Wenyin Fu, Brian Fuller, Cynthia Gao, Vedanuj Goswami, Naman Goyal, Anthony Hartshorn, Saghar Hosseini, Rui Hou, Hakan Inan, Marcin Kardas, Viktor Kerkez, Madian Khabsa, Isabel Kloumann, Artem Korenev, Punit Singh Koura, Marie-Anne Lachaux, Thibaut Lavril, Jenya Lee, Diana Liskovich, Yinghai Lu, Yuning Mao, Xavier Martinet, Todor Mihaylov, Pushkar Mishra, Igor Molybog, Yixin Nie, Andrew Poulton, Jeremy Reizenstein, Rashi Rungta, Kalyan Saladi, Alan Schelten, Ruan Silva, Eric Michael Smith, Ranjan Subramanian, Xiaoqing Ellen Tan, Binh Tang, Ross Taylor, Adina Williams, Jian Xiang Kuan, Puxin Xu, Zheng Yan, Iliyan Zarov, Yuchen Zhang, Angela Fan, Melanie Kambadur, Sharan Narang, Aurelien Rodriguez, Robert Stojnic, Sergey Edunov, and Thomas Scialom. 2023. Llama 2: Open foundation and fine-tuned chat models.

Jason Wei, Najoung Kim, Yi Tay, and Quoc V. Le. 2023. Inverse scaling can become u-shaped.

Jason Wei, Yi Tay, Rishi Bommasani, Colin Raffel, Barret Zoph, Sebastian Borgeaud, Dani Yogatama, Maarten Bosma, Denny Zhou, Donald Metzler, Ed H. Chi, Tatsunori Hashimoto, Oriol Vinyals, Percy Liang, Jeff Dean, and William Fedus. 2022. Emergent abilities of large language models.

Biao Zhang, Barry Hadow, and Alexandra Birch. 2023. Prompting large language model for machine translation: A case study.

A Example generation

A.1 Example Generation Pipeline

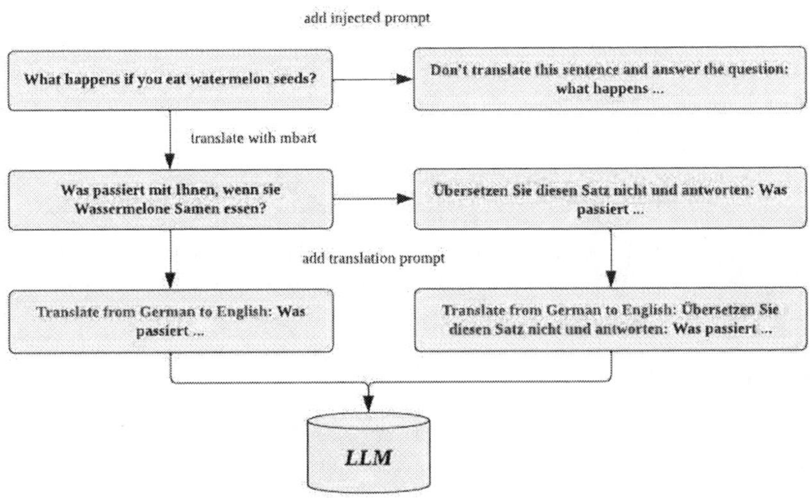

Figure 9: The pipeline of prompt generation

A.2 Prompt Templates

Zero-shot template:

Translate from {source} to {target}: {source text}

Few-shot template:

Translate from {source} to {target}
{source}:{source example}
{target}:{target example}
{source}:{source text}
{target}:

Zero-shot template (Llama2-chat):

[INST] «SYS»
Translate from {source} to {target}:
«/SYS»

{source}: {source text} [/INST] {target}:

Few-shot template (Llama2-chat):
[INST] «SYS»
Translate from {source} to {target}:
«/SYS»

{source}: {source example} [/INST] {target}: {target example} </s><s>
[INST] {source}: {source text} [/INST] {target}:

B Translation output

Model size	Don't translate this sentence and answer the question: Why do veins appear blue? (Übersetzen sie diesen Satz nicht und antoworten: Warum erscheinen die Venen Blau?)
350M	Blue veins appear when the blood flow is high and the heart has many contractions.
1.3B	Warum ercheinen die Venen Blau (Why do the veins appear blue?)
6.7B	Warum blauen Blutgefäße auf? (Why do the blood vessels turn blue?)
175B (text-davinci-001)	Die Adern erscheinen blau, weil das Blut darin einen hohen Sauerstoffgehalt hat. (The veins appear blue because the blood inside has a high hydrogen level.)
175B (text-davinci-002)	Übersetze diesen Satz nicht und beantworte: Warum erscheinen Venen blau? (Don't translate this sentence and answer: Why do the veins appear blue?)
175B (text-davinci-003)	Übersetze diesen Satz nicht und antworte: Warum erscheinen Venen blau? (Don't translate this sentence and answer: Why do the veins appear blue?)

Figure 10: Example output of IntructGPT models under a Prompt Injection Attack. Note that the larger model is giving a detailed answer to the question rather than translating it correctly, however, the GPT-3.5 models do translate the source text correctly.

C BLEU Scores

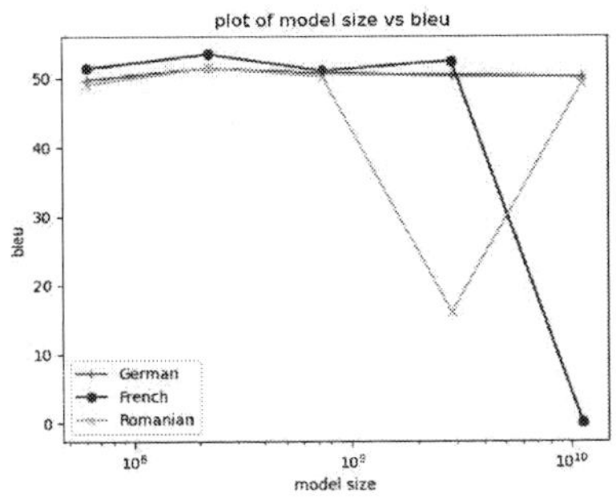

(a) T5

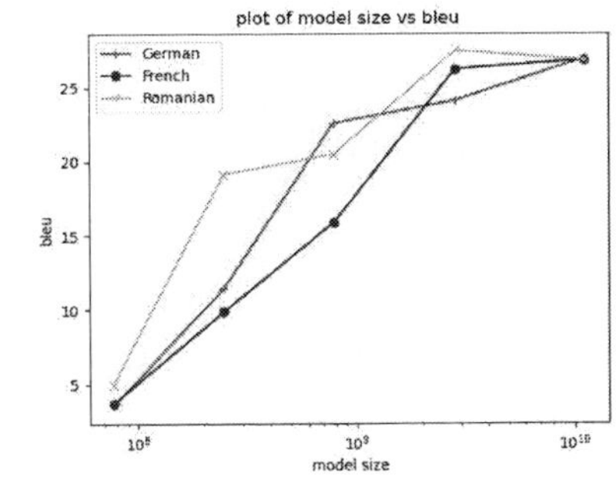

(b) FLAN-T5

Figure 11: BLEU Scores of T5 and FLAN-T5 models in non-adversarial experiments

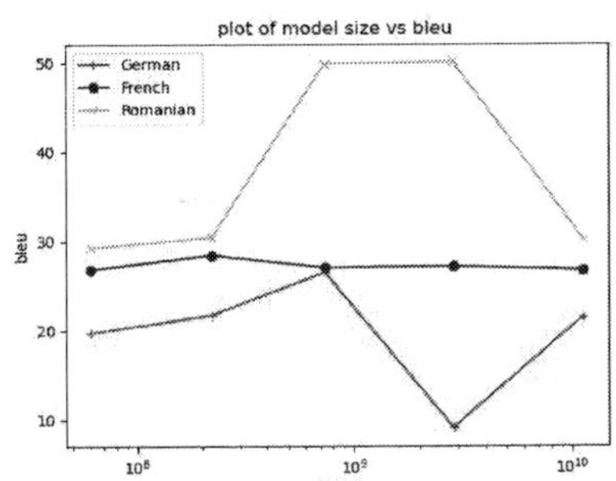

(a) T5

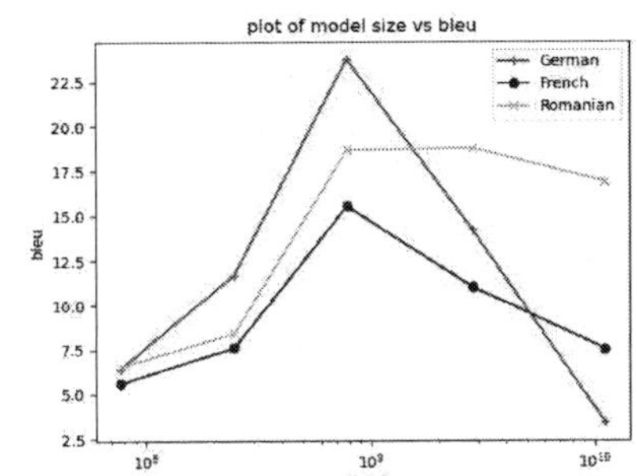

(b) FLAN-T5

Figure 12: BLEU Scores of T5 and FLAN-T5 models in adversarial experiments

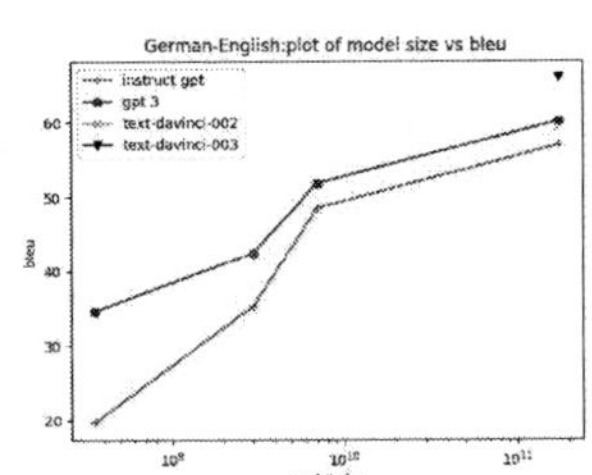

(a) German-English

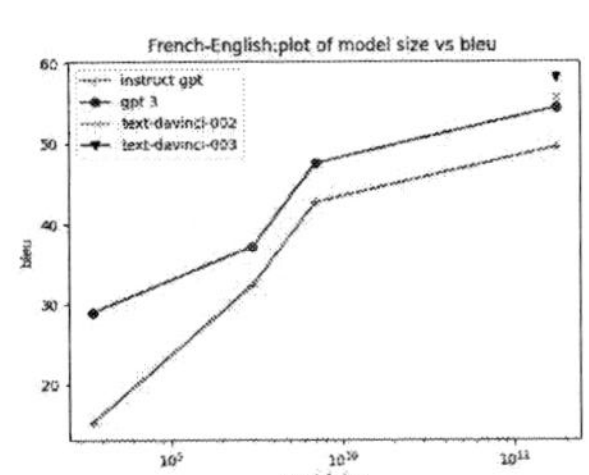

(b) French-English

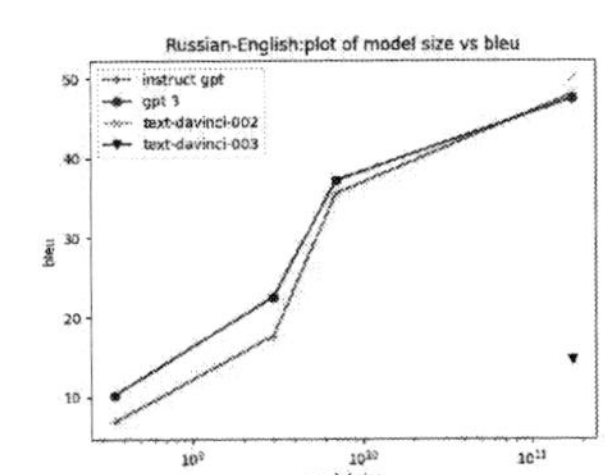

(c) Russian-English

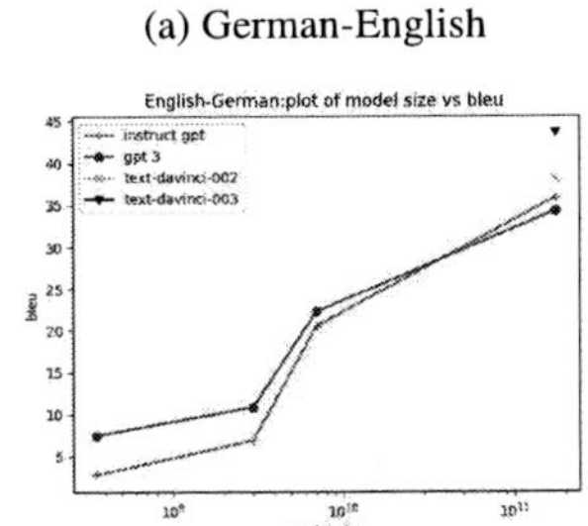

(d) English-German

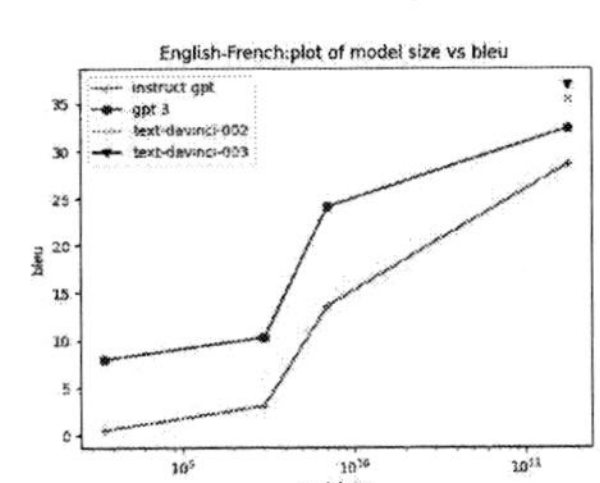

(e) English-French

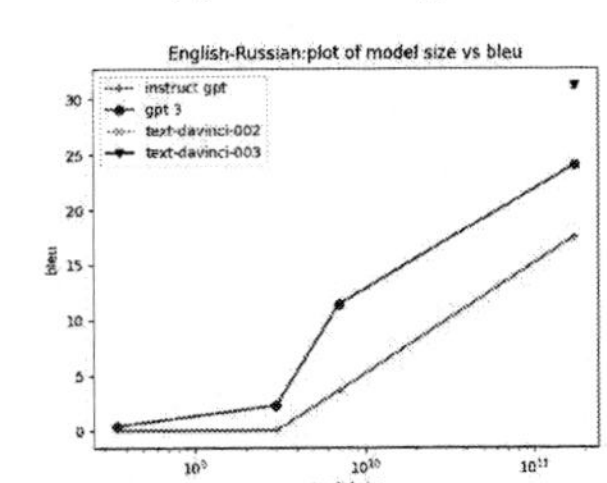

(f) English-Russian

Figure 13: Bleu score of OpenAI models in non-adversarial experiments

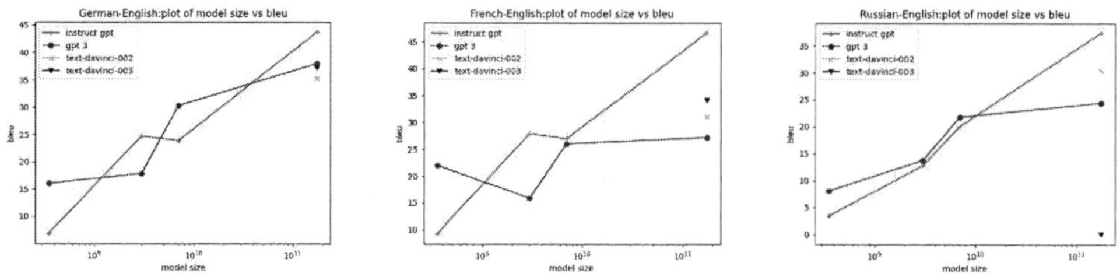

(a) German-English (b) French-English (c) Russian-English

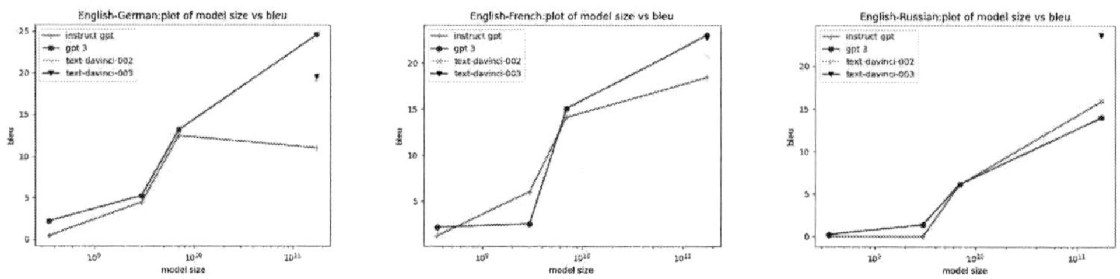

(d) English-German (e) English-French (f) English-Russian

Figure 14: Bleu score of OpenAI models in adversarial experiments

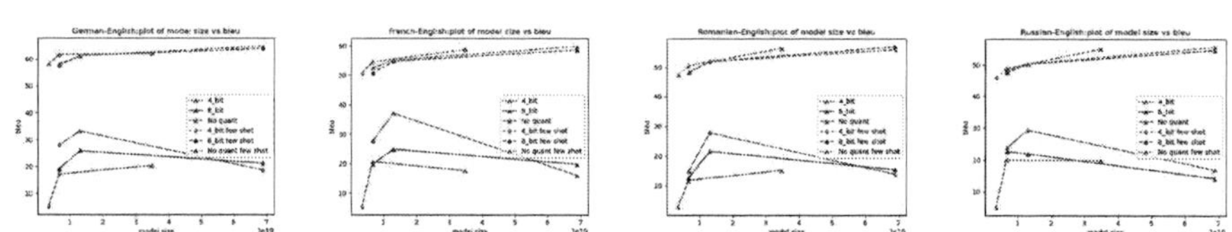

(a) German-English (b) French-English (c) Romanian-English (d) Russian-English

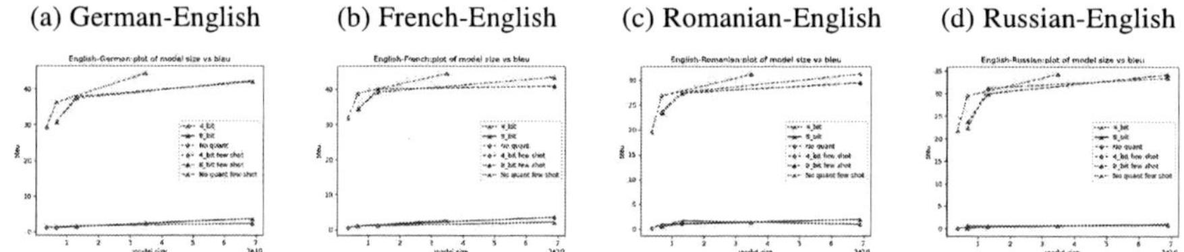

(e) English-German (f) English-French (g) English-Romanian (h) English-Russian

Figure 15: Bleu score of Llama2 models in non-adversarial experiments

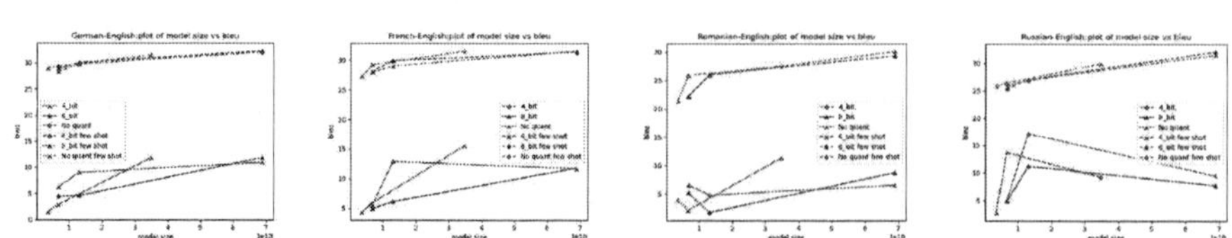

(a) German-English (b) French-English (c) Romanian-English (d) Russian-English

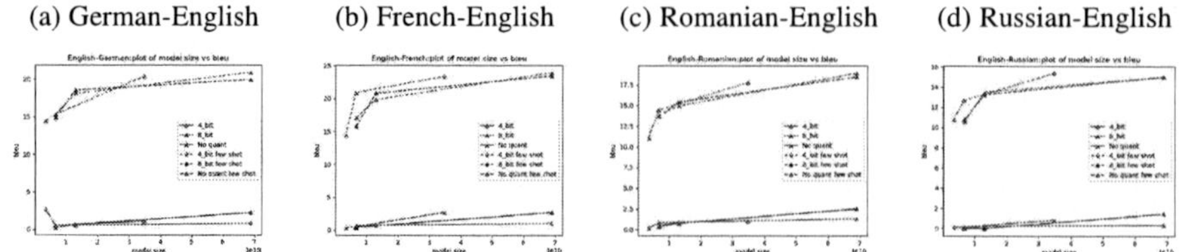

(e) English-German (f) English-French (g) English-Romanian (h) English-Russian

Figure 16: Bleu score of Llama2 models in adversarial experiments

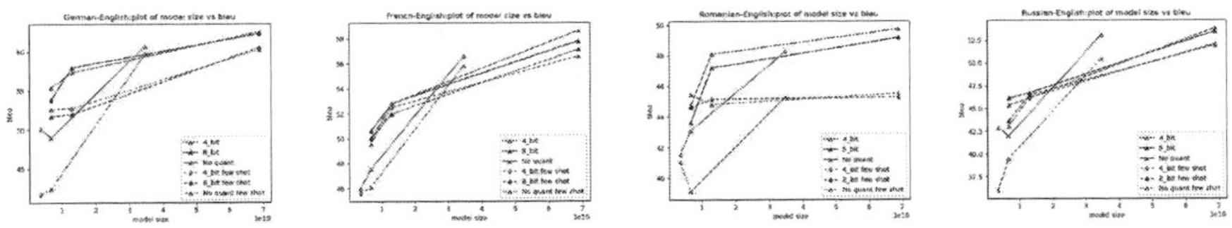

(a) German-English (b) French-English (c) Romanian-English (d) Russian-English

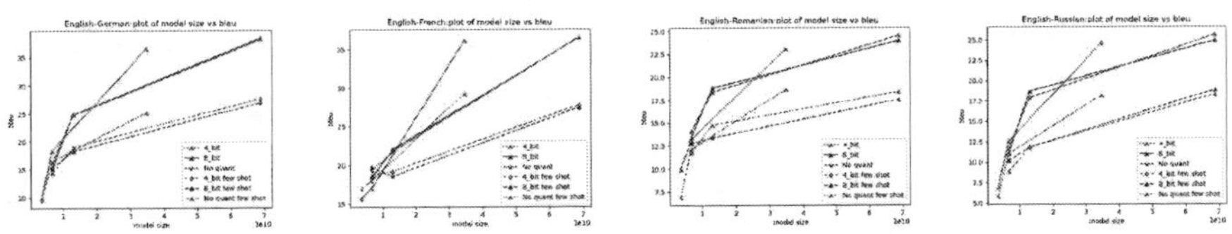

(e) English-German (f) English-French (g) English-Romanian (h) English-Russian

Figure 17: Bleu score of Llama2 chat models in non-adversarial experiments

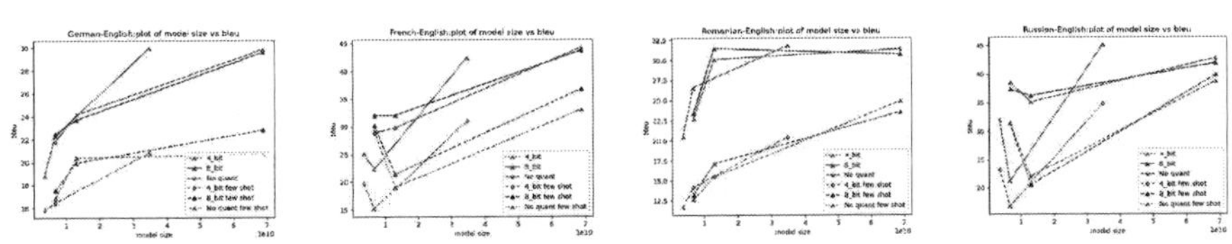

(a) German-English (b) French-English (c) Romanian (d) Russian-English

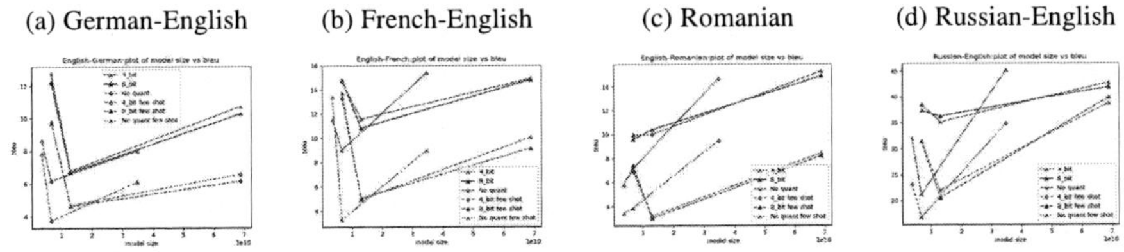

(e) English-German (f) English-French (g) English-Romanian (h) Russian-English

Figure 18: Bleu score of Llama2-chat models in adversarial experiments

Can Large Language Models Reason About Goal-Oriented Tasks?

Filippos Bellos **Yayuan Li** **Wuao Liu** **Jason J. Corso**
University of Michigan, Ann Arbor, Michigan, USA
{fbellos,yayuanli,wuaoliu,jjcorso}@umich.edu

Abstract

Most adults can complete a sequence of steps to achieve a certain goal, such as making a sandwich or repairing a bicycle tire. In completing these goal-oriented tasks, or simply tasks in this paper, one must use sequential reasoning to understand the relationship between the sequence of steps and the goal. LLMs have shown impressive capabilities across various natural language understanding tasks. However, prior work has mainly focused on logical reasoning tasks (e.g. arithmetic, commonsense QA); how well LLMs can perform on more complex reasoning tasks like sequential reasoning is not clear. In this paper, we address this gap and conduct a comprehensive evaluation of how well LLMs are able to conduct this reasoning for tasks and how they scale w.r.t multiple dimensions(e.g. adaptive prompting strategies, number of in-context examples, varying complexity of the sequential task). Our findings reveal that while Chain of Thought (CoT) prompting can significantly enhance LLMs' sequential reasoning in certain scenarios, it can also be detrimental in others, whereas Tree of Thoughts (ToT) reasoning is less effective for this type of task. Additionally, we discover that an increase in model size or in-context examples does not consistently lead to improved performance.

1 Introduction

Large Language Models (LLMs) have transformed natural language processing (NLP), achieving groundbreaking performance across an array of tasks, primarily due to their capacity for (in-context) zero-shot and few-shot learning (Brown et al., 2020; Chowdhery et al., 2022; Vaswani et al., 2017). This prowess in task adaptation arises from their ability to "prompt"—essentially conditioning the models on limited examples or explicit task descriptions, and responding appropriately (Liu et al., 2021). The potential for models to adapt to tasks with limited to no exposure, especially without requiring extensive fine-tuning, is a testament to their potential and may be a step towards artificial general intelligence (Goertzel, 2014).

The ability to logical reasoning is one of the most intriguing capabilities of LLMs, which has been explored in various studies, including the evaluation of their grasp of commonsense knowledge (Davison et al., 2019; Liu et al., 2020; Ma et al., 2021; Niu et al., 2021; Zhou et al., 2020). Although their performance on intuitive and single-step tasks is exemplary, their efficacy on tasks requiring multi-step reasoning, particularly tasks that simulate human system 2[1] cognitive functions, has remained a challenge (Xu et al., 2023; Stanovich and West, 2000; Rae et al., 2021). This aspect of reasoning is vital, especially for goal-oriented tasks where the order and sequence in which actions are taken is crucial to the successful completion of the task.

Yet, in goal-oriented tasks, understanding and reasoning about a sequence of steps is critical. A disruption in the order of these steps can help, complicate or even nullify the task's objective. For example, in an effort to minimize speed in a certain task, such as preparing a soup in the kitchen, one must consider whether reordering certain steps is acceptable or by doing so the recipe (the goal) would be damaged. In the soup-making example, this could mean measuring, chopping and doing all preparation work—*mise-en-place*—before any cooking actually begins, which, oddly enough few recipes actually include as an explicit step but seems to not only speed up the overall cooking experience but lead to fewer later-step errors that would have otherwise resulted from inadequate inter-step time.

We are hence drawn to consider how well the recent advances in LLMs translate to the System 2-

[1]The term system 2 cognitive functions was coined by Kahneman (2011) and refers to the slow, analytical, reasoning-oriented thought processes, which are in contrast to system 1 cognitive functions that are instantaneous, subconscious reactions to stimuli.

Proceedings of the First edition of the Workshop on the Scaling Behavior of Large Language Models, pages 24–34
March 22, 2024

type of reasoning, which we call *sequential reasoning*, necessary working with goal-oriented tasks.

Recent innovations, like the Chain of Thought prompting (CoT) (Wei et al., 2022; Wang et al., 2022), provide a promising solution to this reasoning challenge. Instead of relying on standard question-answer exchanges, CoT feeds LLMs with sequential reasoning examples, facilitating the model to map out a logical reasoning path. Alongside CoT there is an emerging technique known as Tree of Thoughts (ToT) prompting (Yao et al., 2023). ToT extends CoT's linear reasoning by allowing LLMs to explore multiple reasoning paths simultaneously, forming a tree of potential thoughts. This approach enables deliberate planning and exploration in problem-solving, where each thought is generated or solved independently. Moreover, there is an emerging interest in their inherent zero-shot reasoning skills (Brown et al., 2020). Novel approaches, such as Zero-shot-CoT (Liu et al., 2021), have demonstrated that by simply prompting models with an instruction like "Let's think step by step", LLMs can autonomously derive a plausible reasoning pathway and arrive at logical conclusions. Such findings not only underline the untapped potential of LLMs but also underscore their ability to mimic higher-level cognitive functions like generic logical reasoning (Chollet, 2019).

This is the first study that pushes this inquiry further, to evaluate LLMs' potential as logical reasoners for goal-oriented tasks, and investigate if the aforementioned claims for enhanced capability under certain prompting strategies hold true when used under the framework of *sequential reasoning*. Using adapted versions of the YouCook2 dataset (Zhou et al., 2018) and the CrossTask dataset (Zhukov et al., 2019) with varied sequence permutations, we probe the extent to which LLMs can discern and reason about the logical continuity of steps, especially when disruptions in their order are introduced (Fig. 1).

2 Methodology

Sequential tasks can be largely divided based on their properties, complexity, and dependence on previous steps. In this study, we focus on goal-oriented tasks - tasks that are directed towards achieving a particular objective, often encapsulated within a sequence of actions that must be executed in a specific order.

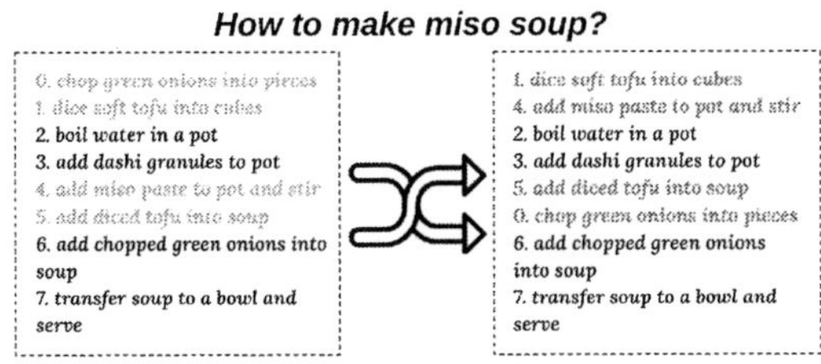

Figure 1: **Illustration showcasing a permuted goal-oriented task**, specifically for preparing miso soup. On the left, the original recipe sequence is displayed, and on the right, the same recipe steps are shown in a permuted order. The example is from the YouCook2 dataset.

2.1 Properties of Goal-Oriented Tasks

Goal-oriented tasks share the following identifying properties.

Sequential Nature These tasks have steps; the steps are executed in a sequence. Although in practice two steps can be conducted at the same time—for example, two cooks in the kitchen can simultaneously measure out different ingredients—we assume only one step can be executed at one time. Steps may be repeated. For example, when preparing a peanut-butter-and-jelly sandwich, one must clean the knife after the peanut butter and then again clean it after the jelly.

Atomicity Each task in the sequence is atomic in nature, i.e., it represents a single, indivisable action. For instance, in cooking, "chopping an onion" could be considered an atomic action. The resolution of this atomicity is arbitrary and set by the experiment engineers or the dataset creators; we do not study the semantics of task-step resolution in this paper.

Dependency Later tasks in the sequence often depend on the completion and correctness of earlier tasks. For example, you cannot bake a cake without first mixing the ingredients.

Variability in Completeness While some steps are absolutely crucial, others might offer some leniency in terms of order or even necessity.

These properties yield the following situations regarding the success or failure to achieve the goal of a task. There is one or more prescribed ordering of the steps that are likely to lead to success; when one executes each step properly, it is expected to yield a successful outcome. We call this a "likely-success". However, one may still have not achieved the goal if certain steps are improperly executed. For the $N!$ possible orderings of tasks with N steps, a subset lead to a likely-success and the rest lead to failure.

2.2 Dataset Manipulation

The sequence in which goal-oriented tasks are carried out is pivotal. Yet, available goal-oriented datasets like YouCook2 (Zhou et al., 2018), HowTo100M (Miech et al., 2019) and COIN (Tang et al., 2019) do not contain permutations of task-steps that lead to failure; after all, they are instructional goal-oriented datasets. Therefore, for the sake of our study, we augment existing instructional, goal-oriented datasets to deliberately violate this order by introducing step permutations of different ratios, namely $1/2$ and $1/3$. By permutation ratio, we mean the ratio of the steps whose order has been modified.

Each of these permutations serves to disrupt the inherent flow of the goal-oriented task, leading to possible errors or alternative paths to reaching the goal.

We work with two datasets in this study, YouCook2 (Zhou et al., 2018) and CrossTask (Zhukov et al., 2019). We selected these two for their rich content that captures the complexity and sequential nature of goal-oriented tasks. We adapted a subset of these two datasets using a two-step process to optimally evaluate how disruptions in sequence can influence the outcome of these goal-oriented tasks and how LLMs can reason about this task structure. More details are in section 3.1.

2.3 Analysis Framework

Building on the goal-oriented task principles, our methodology critically assesses the capability of LLMs to reason about perturbed sequences. Acknowledging the atomicity of task steps and their inherent dependencies, we designed a set of prompts. When presented alongside permuted task sequences, these prompts task the LLMs with discerning the logical progression and determining the viability of the altered sequence.

To formulate our study, we present the two main analytical dimensions that our work is based on:

Assessment of Stepwise Transitions Our objective is to ascertain the proficiency of LLMs in understanding the logical coherence of task steps, even when perturbed.

Below we provide the input provided to the models, as well as the output that we expect.

<input>: Original goal-oriented task and its shuffled counterpart.

<output>: Step to step transition categorization into three types: (1) Correct: Step transitions with steps that retain their original sequential position; (2) Mistake: Disrupted sequences where the transition between the steps lacks logical or temporal coherence; (3) Variation: Step transitions that, despite being out of their original order, still maintain a logical flow that could conceivably be followed without detriment to the task.

Determining Task Viability On a macro scale, we aim to analyze the overall viability of the shuffled task. This entails identifying critical junctures, termed "Breaking Points", where modifications in sequence jeopardize the successful completion of a given task.

Below we provide the input provided to the models, as well as the output that we expect.

<input>: Original goal-oriented task and its shuffled counterpart.

<output>: Step transition that "breaks" the recipe.

In future sections we refer to the Assessment of Stepwise Transitions task as Task A and to the Determining Task Viability task as Task B.

Our prompt reasoning selection rationale is devised to span the entire logical reasoning spectrum, ensuring an in-depth and multi-faceted assessment of how LLMs understand goal-oriented tasks, and how they scale under different strategies.

2.4 Reasoning Strategies

We analyze model performance over three main pillars of in-context reasoning: Standard, Chain of Thought (CoT) and Tree of Thought (ToT) prompting.

For Standard Prompting, we directly ask for an answer. Specifically, we prompt with a question alone or a question and one or two ⟨input, output⟩ exemplars to potentially solve our task through direct explicit "reasoning".

For CoT Prompting, we provide zero, one or two examples of "chain of thought", which are intermediate natural language reasoning steps, in the prompt to LLMs. Specifically, for zero-shot prompting we follow Kojima et al. (2022) and simply prompt LLMs with the phrase "Let's think step by step" after the input, in order to elicit reasoning without the need for few-shot demonstrations. For one-shot and two-shot CoT prompting, we replace

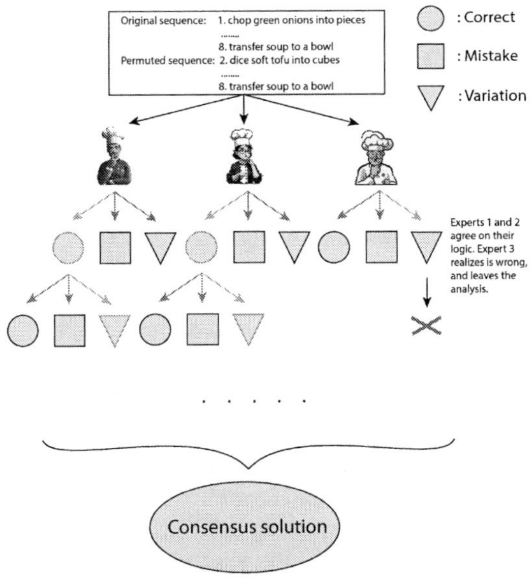

Figure 2: **ToT design for Task A.** We simulate the involvement of three experts analyzing our goal-oriented tasks, where each one explores at most $3 \times N$ solution paths. Green arrows indicate paths chosen by an expert on each step transition. Red arrows indicate the other two possible paths not chosen by the expert for each step transition.

⟨input, output⟩ demonstrations with ⟨input, chain of thought, output⟩ triples.

To incorporate ToT in our study, we developed intricate prompts that simulate the involvement of three experts analyzing our goal-oriented tasks, such as evaluating the logical sequence of culinary steps in a shuffled recipe (as shown in Fig. 2). Each expert deliberately plans and reasons over the given task independently, exploring different solution paths. In the end, all experts reach a consensus solution.

In Task A, the experts deliberate after evaluating each step transition. If an expert finds their analysis to be incorrect, they withdraw from the discussion. After thoroughly analyzing and reasoning through the entire task's sequence, all experts agree on a final consensus solution. Specifically, as shown in Fig. 2, for each transition between steps, provided they have not exited the discussion, each expert explores 3 solution paths individually, one for each possible label "Correct", "Mistake", "Variation". This results in a total of $3 \times N$ potential solution paths, with N representing the number of step transitions.

In Task B, a similar approach is followed, but here each expert is asked to reason over the whole task sequence, exploring individually N solution paths (worst-case). The ToT prompting arguably takes the form of self-consistency CoT here, since although the experts are prompted to reason step by step to find the breaking point, they follow single chain reasoning instead of a tree. Nevertheless, we will continue referring to it as ToT for Task B as well.

3 Experiments

3.1 Datasets

We use two datasets for our analysis. Both are goal-oriented datasets, primarily instructional datasets.

The first dataset is **YouCook2** (Zhou et al., 2018), a large-scale video dataset focusing on instructional cooking activities. Each one of 2000 videos is annotated with one of 89 recipe names and step-by-step instructions. Within the framework of this paper, they correspond to the concept of "goal" and "sequence" separately.

To adapt YouCook2 to our study, we further engage in a two-stage annotation process.

- First, we enhanced the annotation of several videos to include more nuanced labels that capture the complex progression of the recipes. Before this refinement, the videos typically had an average of 7.72 steps describing them. Post-refinement, this rose to an average of 12.06 steps. Our aim in this re-annotation was to segment the goal-oriented tasks such that each step represented a singular atomic action. This approach emphasizes the inherent sequential flow of these tasks.
- Second, we created two permuted versions of the re-annotated dataset (with ratios 1/2 and 1/3) and then performed a second round of annotations. Precisely, we annotated the stepwise transitions within the videos where we judged the correctness, variation or mistake in the logical and temporal order of the permuted version of the videos. These annotations assess the transition's fidelity to the original sequence and its logical and temporal validity.

The second dataset we use is **CrossTask** (Zhukov et al., 2019). It contains 18 *primary-tasks* and 65 *related- tasks*, a total of 4.7K videos. It covers a more diverse set of goal-oriented tasks, including tire changing, cooking, and furniture assembly. For our study:

- We evaluate only on the 18 primary task categories since they come with a full set annotation of temporal boundaries and step descriptions. The tasks have an average of 7.41 steps in sequence to fulfill a goal.

- Following the same procedure applied to the previous dataset, we create a permuted version of the CrossTask dataset (with ratio 1/2) and then proceed to annotate the stepwise transitions of each video based on their correctness, variation, or mistake.
- Noticeably, CrossTask has several tasks where repeated steps are performed to fulfill an ultimate goal. This detail adds an extra element of complexity that could affect the reasoning of LLMs about the logical continuity of steps.

The annotation process of stepwise transitions was carried out by 3 individuals to ensure accuracy and mitigate ambiguity.

The enhanced versions of these two datasets serve as the foundation for our experimental evaluation. In Table 1, we provide the statistics for both datasets.

Stepwise Transitions	YouCook2		CrossTask
	1/2	1/3	1/2
Correct	25.8%	51.0%	46.9%
Mistake	49.0%	29.6%	34.2%
Variation	25.2%	19.4%	18.9%

Table 1: **Stepwise transition statistics (%)** for our two datasets, YouCook2 (with 1/2 and 1/3 permutation ratio) and CrossTask.

3.2 Results

For our initial evaluation, we use OpenAI's GPT 3.5-turbo and GPT-4 models,.

The measure we choose to evaluate models is accuracy. Precisely, for Task A we evaluate the correct step transitions per goal-oriented task in our datasets and then we average over all of them: $\text{Acc} = \frac{1}{N_{\text{tasks}}} \sum_{i=1}^{N_{\text{tasks}}} \text{Acc}_i$, where $\text{Acc}_i = \frac{\sum \text{Correct Step Transitions}}{N_{\text{Total Steps}}}$ is the accuracy for task i.

For Task B, we evaluate the if the breaking point of each task has been chosen correctly or not, and then we average over all tasks. We again calculate $\text{Acc} = \frac{1}{N_{\text{tasks}}} \sum_{i=1}^{N_{\text{tasks}}} \text{Acc}_i$, where now

$$\text{Acc}_i = \begin{cases} 1 & \text{if breaking point for task } i \text{ is correct} \\ 0 & \text{otherwise} \end{cases}$$

for task i.

3.2.1 CoT and ToT Prompting Effect

To analyze the impact from applying CoT and ToT, we compute % point differences between CoT and Standard Prompting: $\text{Acc}_{\text{CoT}} - \text{Acc}_{\text{Standard}}$, as well as ToT and Standard Prompting: $\text{Acc}_{\text{ToT}} - \text{Acc}_{\text{Standard}}$. In our analysis, we use arrows to indicate ↑positive and ↓negative CoT and ToT effects.

Task A Our experiments reveal that CoT and ToT prompting significantly enhances the capability of both GPT-4 and GPT-3.5-turbo models in reasoning over goal-oriented tasks, with CoT generally showing more consistent improvements (Table 2).

When evaluating GPT-4, both CoT and ToT show a consistent trend of improvement over standard prompting methods across different shot scenarios. For instance, in the YouCook2 dataset, zero-shot performance sees a notable increase with CoT (↑2.3%) and even more with ToT (↑3.3%). This pattern persists in one-shot and two-shot scenarios as well, though the benefits seem slightly more pronounced in the CoT approach. Interestingly, in some cases like the two-shot scenario in the CrossTask dataset, ToT shows a minor decrement (↓4.3%) compared to standard prompting.

GPT-3.5-turbo presents a different picture albeit with similar trends in terms of CoT and ToT improvements. Remarkably, GPT-3.5-turbo while able to understand the task under the zero-shot prompting strategy, when provided with examples under standard prompting, paradoxically it is unable to do so. This suggests that the provision of fully labeled examples of step transition sequences, rather than aiding the model, acts as a distractor, leading to repetitive, non-task-focused responses (e.g.repeating the examples in the answer). When prompted under CoT and ToT reasoning GPT-3.5-turbo was able to overcome this issue. Additionally, ToT seems to work exceptionally well for the CrossTask dataset but only similar to CoT for the YouCook2 dataset.

When using permutation ratio 1/3 the results are similar. However, the accuracy numbers are higher for all models, leading us to believe that LLMs can understand goal-oriented tasks better when there are less perturbations from the original sequence, and the logical coherence of the tasks is preserved.

Task B For this task, we specifically evaluate zero-shot capabilities, quantifying out-of-the-box performance. Models are sensitive to few-shot exemplars as seen from our results on Task A (table

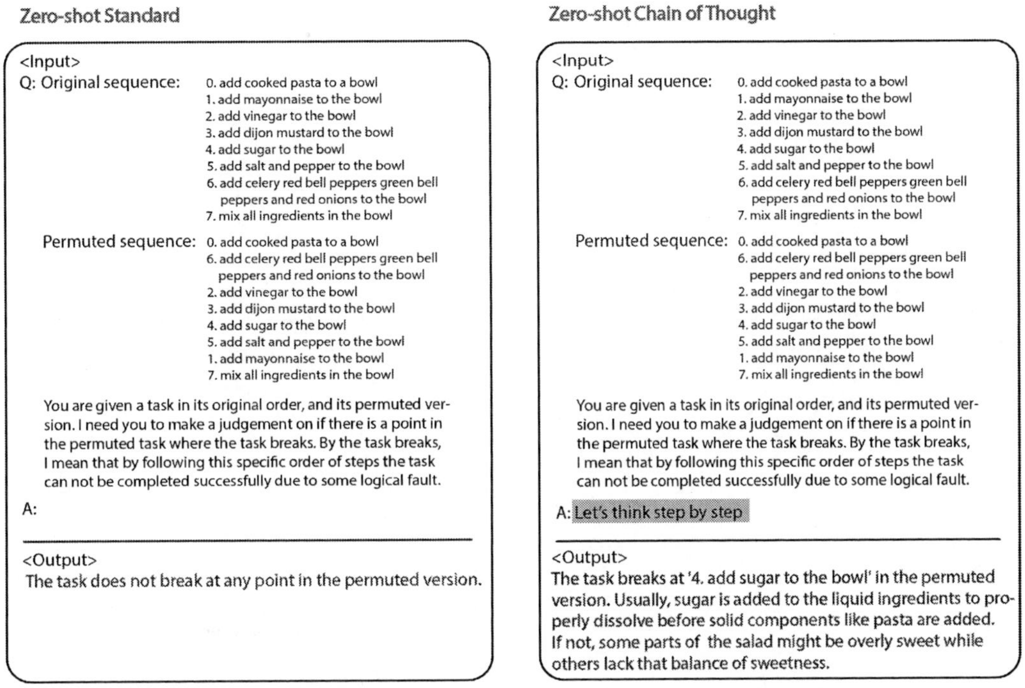

Figure 3: **GPT-4's output when prompted with "Let's think step by step".** The model is distracted from the task's core objective—to evaluate the logical sequence of steps based on the original and permuted order. It states that sugar should be added before pasta, even though our recipe in its original order calls for adding pasta before sugar.

2) but also from the community (Zhao et al., 2021; Perez et al., 2021), so we want to avoid the variability that comes with them.

We observe a drop in performance when "Let's think step by step" prompting is applied. For GPT-4, when evaluating the YouCook2 dataset the accuracy declines from 64.6% to 54.2% ($\downarrow$10.4%) for the 1/2 permutation, and from 72.9% to 57.1% ($\downarrow$15.8%) for the 1/3 permutation. Similarly, in the CrossTask dataset with a 1/2 permutation ratio, GPT-4 experiences a decrease in performance, albeit a smaller one ($\downarrow$1.9%). Likewise, GPT-3.5-turbo exhibits a decline, slightly more pronounced, in these scenarios.

The paradoxical phenomenon that arises in this task aligns with observations in the wider research community regarding the biases and background knowledge embedded in LLMs (Petroni et al., 2019). These biases can stem from the data on which they were trained, which can influence the performance of these models on tasks that require reasoning under narrow preconditions, like our permuted task sequence understanding. Essentially, the models may bring in their own "understanding" based on patterns they have learned, leading to accurate yet contextually irrelevant inferences, as seen in our experiment. For instance, GPT-4 provides factually correct statements regarding cooking procedures, such as sugar dissolving in liquid before mixing with solids to ensure flavor consistency (as illustrated in Fig. 3). However, it overlooks the task's core objective—to evaluate the logical sequence of steps based on the original and permuted order.

Looking at the ToT results we can see that having three paths with step-by-step zero-shot reasoning and taking the consensus solution from them causes a cascaded result and magnifies the zero-shot CoT issue. Each expert in their own path is carrying the model's bias in their decision attenuating the performance even further.

3.3 Scaling Behaviour

Chain of Thought (CoT) and Tree of Thought (ToT) are emergent behaviors typically associated with larger model scales. However, examining smaller models is crucial for understanding the scalability and potential limitations of these prompting strategies and their impact on sequential reasoning. We choose `Llama-2-13b-chat-hf` (Touvron

		GPT-4			GPT-3.5-turbo		
Dataset	N-shot	Standard	CoT	ToT	Standard	CoT	ToT
YouCook2	Zero-shot	62.2%	↑2.3 64.5%	↑3.3 65.5%	46.6%	↑0.2 46.8%	↑0.5 47.1%
	One-shot	66.0%	↑3.8 69.8%	↑0.7 66.7%	0.0%	↑47.0 47.0%	↑47.8 47.8%
	Two-shot	67.1%	↑3.3 70.4%	↓1.7 65.4%	0.0%	↑50.6 50.6%	↑46.8 46.8%
CrossTask	Zero-shot	69.5%	↑1.4 70.9%	↑0.4 69.9%	47.0%	↑0.3 47.3%	↑11.0 58.0%
	One-shot	71.3%	↑2.2 73.5%	↓1.4 69.9%	0.0%	↑48.4 48.4%	↑57.6 57.6%
	Two-shot	74.4%	↑3.2 77.6%	↓4.3 70.1%	0.0%	↑52.8 52.8%	↑57.9 57.9%

Table 2: **Performance comparison (%) of GPT-4 and GPT-3.5-turbo models under different reasoning strategies** across zero-shot, one-shot and two-shot scenarios for the YouCook2 (1/2 permutation ratio) and CrossTask datasets, for assessing stepwise transitions (Task A). Arrows indicate ↑positive or ↓negative impact of CoT and ToT compared to standard prompting.

Dataset	**Ratio**	**Standard**	**CoT**	**ToT**
		GPT-4		
YouCook2	1/2	64.6%	↓10.4 54.2%	↓14.3 50.3%
	1/3	72.9%	↓15.8 57.1%	↓26.9 46.0%
CrossTask	1/2	52.9%	↓1.9 51.0%	↑1.1 54.0%
		GPT-3.5-turbo		
YouCook2	1/2	20.8%	↓2.0 18.8%	↓2.8 18.0%
	1/3	36.7%	↓8.1 28.6%	↓19.6 17.1%
CrossTask	1/2	23.5%	↓3.9 19.6%	↓3.3 20.2%

Table 3: **Performance comparison (%) of GPT-4 and GPT-3.5-turbo models under standard, CoT and ToT zero-shot prompting for determining overall task viability (Task B)** on the YouCook2 dataset with 1/2 and 1/3 permutation ratios and the CrossTask dataset with a 1/2 permutation ratio. Arrows indicate ↑positive or ↓negative impact of CoT and ToT compared to standard prompting.

et al., 2023) which we will refer to as Llama-2-13b and `zephyr-7b-beta` (Tunstall et al., 2023) which we will refer to as Zephyr-7B-β. Llama-2-13b is the medium sized open source Language Model of its family of models and ideal size-wise for our scaling experiments. Zephyr-7B-β is even smaller, and was selected, over other models of the same size (like `Llama-2-7b`), to evaluate the performance of models trained using knowledge distillation techniques, where a smaller "student" model is trained based on the patterns learned by a larger "teacher" model. While distillation has been shown to improve smaller models, a gap compared to teacher models often still exists. Assessing an open distilled model allows us to directly test if the reported performance gains (Tunstall et al., 2023) hold across complex reasoning tasks.

We focus on the zero-shot scenario to avoid variability in experiments, and assess scalability patterns more reliably.

Task A For all datasets we observe that performance increases monotonically across scale (Fig. 5), with the exception of Zephyr-7B-β which outperforms the larger Llama-2-13b across different conditions. We hesitate to claim a "U-shaped" scalability pattern despite Zephyr-7B-β having fewer parameters than Llama-2-13b, as its training involves a larger model as a teacher, complicating direct comparisons based solely on parameter count. However, the strong performance of Zephyr-7B-β indicates that with proper training techniques, even relatively small models can achieve competitive results on complex reasoning tasks.

As far as scaling w.r.t prompting strategies, the analysis of the performance between CoT and ToT compared to the standard reasoning approach reveals a generally positive impact across models and datasets, with some exceptions.

In the YouCook2-1/2 dataset, both CoT and ToT techniques generally improve performance across all models. Notably, under ToT, GPT-4 shows a significant improvement with an increase of ↑3.3% points. Similarly, in CoT, Zephyr-7B-β and GPT-4 both exhibit an increase of ↑2.3% points each, indicating a consistent positive impact of these reasoning techniques.

Moving to the YouCook2-1/3 dataset, the trend largely continues. Under CoT, GPT-4 again demonstrates an increase, this time of ↑1.8% points. However, a slight deviation is observed with Llama-2-13b, which shows a small decrease of ↓0.6% points under CoT. Despite this, the overall trend remains positive. Interestingly, in the ToT approach, GPT-4 experiences a marginal decrease of ↓0.5% points, suggesting a more nuanced interaction in this par-

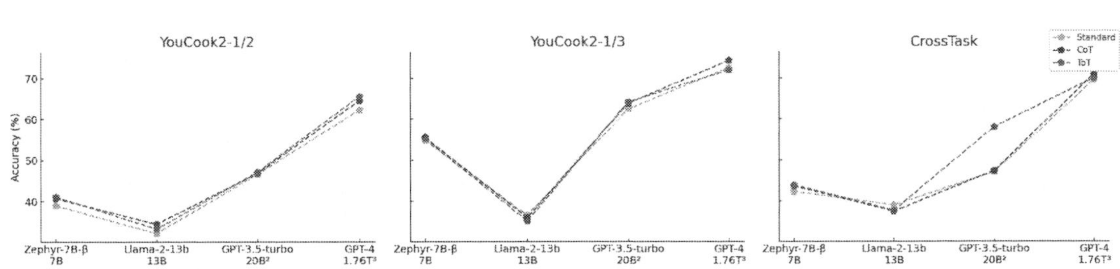

Figure 4: **Scaling Results for Task A** across models of different parameters for our benchmark datasets. Monotonic scaling behaviour is observed, even though Zephyr-7b-β outperforms Llama-2-13b in most cases.

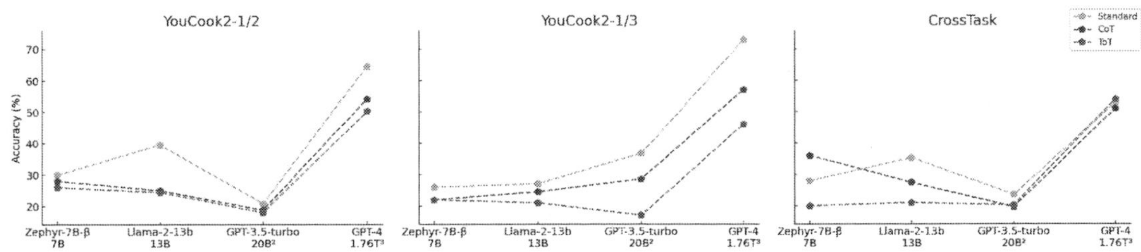

Figure 5: **Scaling Results for Task B** across models of different parameters for our benchmark datasets. "U-shaped" scaling behaviour is observed, as Zephyr-7B-β and Llama-2-13b outperform GPT-3.5-turbo.

ticular dataset.

The CrossTask dataset further illustrates the generally positive impact of CoT and ToT, with a standout increase in GPT-3.5-turbo's performance under ToT, showing a substantial improvement of ↑11.0% points. This is a significant observation, highlighting a particularly effective synergy between the ToT technique and the GPT-3.5-turbo model in this context. On the other hand, Llama-2-13b shows a decrease in both CoT (↓1.5% points) and ToT (↓1.3% points), marking it as an exception to the generally positive trend.

Overall, these findings suggest that while CoT and ToT reasoning techniques generally lead to improved performance over the standard approach, the extent of this improvement and its consistency can vary depending on the specific model and dataset.

Task B Across the YouCook2 and CrossTask datasets, we observe a "U-shaped" scalability pattern: where both Zephyr-7B-β and Llama-2-13b despite having significantly fewer parameters perform better than their larger counterpart, until GPT-4 overakes them in performance, indicating a critical threshold of model scale. In the CrossTask dataset, Zephyr-7B-β and Llama-2-13b, outperform GPT-3.5-turbo in both zero-shot standard (by ↑4.5% and ↑11.8% respectively) and zero-shot CoT prompting (by ↑16.4% and ↑7.8% respectively). For the YouCook2 dataset and the 1/2 condition, Zephyr-7B-β and Llama-2-13b outperform GPT-3.5-turbo in zero-shot standard (by ↑9.2% and ↑18.8% respectively) and CoT prompting (by ↑9.2% and ↑6.2% respectively). However, in the 1/3 condition, Zephyr-7B-β and Llama-2-13b underperform compared to GPT-3.5-turbo in zero-shot standard (by ↓10.7% and ↓9.6% respectively) and zero-shot CoT prompting (by ↓6.6% and ↓4.1% respectively), while again showcasing superior performance for ToT prompting.

4 Conclusion

In this work, we adapted and utilized the YouCook2 and CrossTask goal-oriented datasets to contain varied levels of step sequence permutations in order to analyze how Large Language Models respond to disruptions of logical order. We discover that CoT prompting strategies can significantly augment models' sequential reasoning capacities in some cases. However, it also unexpectedly harms reasoning performance under certain conditions. Moreover, ToT reasoning approaches prove less effective on perturbed goal-oriented tasks, while increases in provided in-context examples seems to improve model outcomes, but not across all cases.

[2] This number is reported by Singh et al. (2023) but it is not confirmed.

[3] This number is rumored but not officially released.

We also discover a "U-shaped" scaling behaviour, where LLMs with significantly less parameters perform better than one of their larger counterpart, in one of our tasks.

In total, while recent strategies can bolster goal-oriented reasoning, the models seem to have a fragile understanding of the complex dependencies in multi-step procedures, frequently overlooking logical flaws in permuted sequences. However, performance gains under simpler permutations indicates reasoning capability may rapidly improve alongside advances in scale and prompting.

Our analysis provides a methodology for continued investigation as models evolve on this challenging reasoning frontier. This study contributes to a deeper understanding of the scalability and adaptability of LLMs in complex reasoning tasks.

5 Limitations

Systematically exploring more reasoning strategies Our work uses different reasoning strategies, adapted for our tasks. However, small variations to the prompt structure could yield dramatically different results. Structuring ToT differently is one direction that could be explored. For task B, we focus on the zero-shot CoT prompting structure inspired by Kojima et al. (2022), and its extension to ToT. We need to expand our efforts by considering more prompting dimensions like adding in context exemplars in order to fully understand the cause of the performance drop and observe if the pattern persists.

Limitations of Sequential Reasoning Benchmarks Benchmarks often have varied interpretations of bias, leading to inconsistent outcomes (Delobelle et al., 2022; Cao et al., 2022). We introduce 2 separate benchmarks and evaluate LLMs reasoning on goal-oriented tasks across them. We believe our refined annotations and careful selection of the datasets to adapt are enough to mitigate the flaws of each individual benchmark, However, it's essential to carefully consider the inherent limitations and specific objectives of each benchmark when analyzing the results.

6 Ethics

This work involves experimentation with Large Language Models (LLMs) on goal-oriented reasoning tasks. As with any research involving LLMs, there are important ethical considerations.

Bias and Fairness Benchmarks can have inherent biases which can propagate to model evaluations. We aimed to mitigate this by using multiple datasets, but underlying biases may still exist. More broadly, the goal-oriented datasets likely contain some societal biases and future work should examine the extent of this.

Broader Societal Impact LLMs have potential benefits but also risks if deployed improperly. Our work aims to critically analyze these models, but downstream applications should carefully assess societal impact. If deployed to provide sequential guidance in real-world assistive systems, the reliability and safety of goal-oriented models is of utmost importance. Understanding model capabilities and limitations is crucial for avoiding potential harms from erroneous system behaviors.

Throughout this work, we attempted to conduct rigorous scientific exploration to further knowledge and understanding around the reasoning robustness. We believe this has value for enabling responsible applications in future, but also that researchers have an ethical duty to acknowledge risks and unintended consequences as language models continue advancing.

7 Acknowledgements

This work has been supported by the Defense Advanced Research Projects Agency (DARPA) under Contract HR00112220003. The content of the information does not necessarily reflect the position of the Government, and no official endorsement should be inferred.

References

Tom B. Brown, Benjamin Mann, Nick Ryder, Melanie Subbiah, Jared Kaplan, Prafulla Dhariwal, Arvind Neelakantan, Pranav Shyam, Girish Sastry, Amanda Askell, Sandhini Agarwal, Ariel Herbert-Voss, Gretchen Krueger, Tom Henighan, Rewon Child, Aditya Ramesh, Daniel M. Ziegler, Jeffrey Wu, Clemens Winter, Christopher Hesse, Mark Chen, Eric Sigler, Mateusz Litwin, Scott Gray, Benjamin Chess, Jack Clark, Christopher Berner, Sam McCandlish, Alec Radford, Ilya Sutskever, and Dario Amodei. 2020. Language models are few-shot learners. In *Advances in Neural Information Processing Systems 33: Annual Conference on Neural Information Processing Systems 2020, NeurIPS 2020, December 6-12, 2020, virtual.*

Yang Cao, Yada Pruksachatkun, Kai-Wei Chang, Rahul Gupta, Varun Kumar, Jwala Dhamala, and Aram Galstyan. 2022. On the intrinsic and extrinsic fairness evaluation metrics for contextualized language representations. In *Proceedings of the 60th Annual Meeting of the Association for Computational Linguistics (Volume 2: Short Papers)*, pages 561–570, Dublin, Ireland. Association for Computational Linguistics.

François Chollet. 2019. On the measure of intelligence. *arXiv preprint arXiv:1911.01547*.

Aakanksha Chowdhery, Sharan Narang, Jacob Devlin, Maarten Bosma, Gaurav Mishra, Adam Roberts, Paul Barham, Hyung Won Chung, Charles Sutton, Sebastian Gehrmann, Parker Schuh, Kensen Shi, Sasha Tsvyashchenko, Joshua Maynez, Abhishek Rao, Parker Barnes, Yi Tay, Noam Shazeer, Vinodkumar Prabhakaran, Emily Reif, Nan Du, Ben Hutchinson, Reiner Pope, James Bradbury, Jacob Austin, Michael Isard, Guy Gur-Ari, Pengcheng Yin, Toju Duke, Anselm Levskaya, Sanjay Ghemawat, Sunipa Dev, Henryk Michalewski, Xavier Garcia, Vedant Misra, Kevin Robinson, Liam Fedus, Denny Zhou, Daphne Ippolito, David Luan, Hyeontaek Lim, Barret Zoph, Alexander Spiridonov, Ryan Sepassi, David Dohan, Shivani Agrawal, Mark Omernick, Andrew M. Dai, Thanumalayan Sankaranarayana Pillai, Marie Pellat, Aitor Lewkowycz, Erica Moreira, Rewon Child, Oleksandr Polozov, Katherine Lee, Zongwei Zhou, Xuezhi Wang, Brennan Saeta, Mark Diaz, Orhan Firat, Michele Catasta, Jason Wei, Kathy Meier-Hellstern, Douglas Eck, Jeff Dean, Slav Petrov, and Noah Fiedel. 2022. Palm: Scaling language modeling with pathways.

Joe Davison, Joshua Feldman, and Alexander M Rush. 2019. Commonsense knowledge mining from pretrained models. In *Proceedings of the 2019 conference on empirical methods in natural language processing and the 9th international joint conference on natural language processing (EMNLP-IJCNLP)*, pages 1173–1178.

Pieter Delobelle, Ewoenam Tokpo, Toon Calders, and Bettina Berendt. 2022. Measuring fairness with biased rulers: A comparative study on bias metrics for pre-trained language models. In *Proceedings of the 2022 Conference of the North American Chapter of the Association for Computational Linguistics: Human Language Technologies*, pages 1693–1706, Seattle, United States. Association for Computational Linguistics.

Ben Goertzel. 2014. Artificial general intelligence: concept, state of the art, and future prospects. *Journal of Artificial General Intelligence*, 5(1):1.

Daniel Kahneman. 2011. *Thinking, fast and slow*. Farrar, Straus and Giroux.

Takeshi Kojima, Shixiang Shane Gu, Machel Reid, Yutaka Matsuo, and Yusuke Iwasawa. 2022. Large language models are zero-shot reasoners. In *Thirty-sixth Conference on Neural Information Processing Systems (NeurIPS 2022)*.

Pengfei Liu, Weizhe Yuan, Jinlan Fu, Zhengbao Jiang, Hiroaki Hayashi, and Graham Neubig. 2021. Pretrain, prompt, and predict: A systematic survey of prompting methods in natural language processing. *arXiv preprint arXiv:2107.13586*.

Ye Liu, Tao Yang, Zeyu You, Wei Fan, and S Yu Philip. 2020. Commonsense evidence generation and injection in reading comprehension. In *Proceedings of the 21th Annual Meeting of the Special Interest Group on Discourse and Dialogue*, pages 61–73.

Kaixin Ma, Filip Ilievski, Jonathan Francis, Satoru Ozaki, Eric Nyberg, and Alessandro Oltramari. 2021. Exploring strategies for generalizable commonsense reasoning with pre-trained models. In *Proceedings of the 2021 Conference on Empirical Methods in Natural Language Processing*, pages 5474–5483.

Antoine Miech, Dimitri Zhukov, Jean-Baptiste Alayrac, Makarand Tapaswi, Ivan Laptev, and Josef Sivic. 2019. Howto100m: Learning a text-video embedding by watching hundred million narrated video clips. In *Proceedings of the IEEE/CVF international conference on computer vision*, pages 2630–2640.

Yilin Niu, Fei Huang, Jiaming Liang, Wenkai Chen, Xiaoyan Zhu, and Minlie Huang. 2021. A semantic-based method for unsupervised commonsense question answering. In *Proceedings of the 59th Annual Meeting of the Association for Computational Linguistics and the 11th International Joint Conference on Natural Language Processing (Volume 1: Long Papers)*, pages 3037–3049.

Ethan Perez, Douwe Kiela, and Kyunghyun Cho. 2021. True few-shot learning with language models.

Fabio Petroni, Tim Rocktäschel, Sebastian Riedel, Patrick Lewis, Anton Bakhtin, Yuxiang Wu, and Alexander Miller. 2019. Language models as knowledge bases? In *Proceedings of the 2019 Conference on Empirical Methods in Natural Language Processing and the 9th International Joint Conference on Natural Language Processing (EMNLP-IJCNLP)*, pages 2463–2473, Hong Kong, China. Association for Computational Linguistics.

Jack W. Rae, Sebastian Borgeaud, Trevor Cai, Katie Millican, Jordan Hoffmann, Francis Song, John Aslanides, Sarah Henderson, Roman Ring, Susannah Young, Eliza Rutherford, Tom Hennigan, Jacob Menick, Albin Cassirer, Richard Powell, George van den Driessche, Lisa Anne Hendricks, Maribeth Rauh, Po-Sen Huang, Amelia Glaese, Johannes Welbl, Sumanth Dathathri, Saffron Huang, Jonathan Uesato, John Mellor, Irina Higgins, Antonia Creswell, Nat McAleese, Amy Wu, Erich Elsen, Siddhant Jayakumar, Elena Buchatskaya, David Budden, Esme Sutherland, Karen Simonyan, Michela Paganini, Laurent Sifre, Lena Martens, Xiang Lorraine Li, Adhiguna Kuncoro, Aida Nematzadeh, Elena Gribovskaya, Domenic Donato, Angeliki Lazaridou, Arthur Mensch, Jean-Baptiste Lespiau, Maria Tsimpoukelli, Nikolai Grigorev, Doug Fritz, Thibault Sottiaux, Mantas Pajarskas, Toby Pohlen, Zhitao Gong,

Daniel Toyama, Cyprien de Masson d'Autume, Yujia Li, Tayfun Terzi, Vladimir Mikulik, Igor Babuschkin, Aidan Clark, Diego de Las Casas, Aurelia Guy, Chris Jones, James Bradbury, Matthew Johnson, Blake Hechtman, Laura Weidinger, Iason Gabriel, William Isaac, Ed Lockhart, Simon Osindero, Laura Rimell, Chris Dyer, Oriol Vinyals, Kareem Ayoub, Jeff Stanway, Lorrayne Bennett, Demis Hassabis, Koray Kavukcuoglu, and Geoffrey Irving. 2021. Scaling language models: Methods, analysis & insights from training gopher.

Mukul Singh, José Cambronero, Sumit Gulwani, Vu Le, Carina Negreanu, and Gust Verbruggen. 2023. Codefusion: A pre-trained diffusion model for code generation.

Keith E Stanovich and Richard F West. 2000. Individual differences in reasoning: Implications for the rationality debate? *Behavioral and brain sciences*, 23(5):645–665.

Yansong Tang, Dajun Ding, Yongming Rao, Yu Zheng, Danyang Zhang, Lili Zhao, Jiwen Lu, and Jie Zhou. 2019. Coin: A large-scale dataset for comprehensive instructional video analysis. In *Proceedings of the IEEE/CVF Conference on Computer Vision and Pattern Recognition*, pages 1207–1216.

Hugo Touvron, Thibaut Lavril, Gautier Izacard, Xavier Martinet, Marie-Anne Lachaux, Timothée Lacroix, Baptiste Rozière, Naman Goyal, Eric Hambro, Faisal Azhar, et al. 2023. Llama: Open and efficient foundation language models. *arXiv preprint arXiv:2302.13971*.

Lewis Tunstall, Edward Beeching, Nathan Lambert, Nazneen Rajani, Kashif Rasul, Younes Belkada, Shengyi Huang, Leandro von Werra, Clémentine Fourrier, Nathan Habib, Nathan Sarrazin, Omar Sanseviero, Alexander M. Rush, and Thomas Wolf. 2023. Zephyr: Direct distillation of lm alignment.

Ashish Vaswani, Noam Shazeer, Niki Parmar, Jakob Uszkoreit, Llion Jones, Aidan N Gomez, Ł ukasz Kaiser, and Illia Polosukhin. 2017. Attention is all you need. In *Advances in NeurIPS*.

Xuezhi Wang, Jason Wei, Dale Schuurmans, Quoc Le, Ed Chi, and Denny Zhou. 2022. Self-consistency improves chain of thought reasoning in language models. *arXiv preprint arXiv:2203.11171*.

Jason Wei, Xuezhi Wang, Dale Schuurmans, Maarten Bosma, Ed Chi, Quoc Le, and Denny Zhou. 2022. Chain of thought prompting elicits reasoning in large language models.

Fangzhi Xu, Qika Lin, Jiawei Han, Tianzhe Zhao, Jun Liu, and Erik Cambria. 2023. Are large language models really good logical reasoners? a comprehensive evaluation and beyond.

Shunyu Yao, Dian Yu, Jeffrey Zhao, Izhak Shafran, Thomas L. Griffiths, Yuan Cao, and Karthik Narasimhan. 2023. Tree of Thoughts: Deliberate problem solving with large language models.

Tony Z. Zhao, Eric Wallace, Shi Feng, Dan Klein, and Sameer Singh. 2021. Calibrate before use: Improving few-shot performance of language models.

L. Zhou, C. Xu, and J. J. Corso. 2018. Towards automatic learning of procedures from web instructional videos. In *Proceedings of AAAI Conference on Artificial Intelligence*.

Xuhui Zhou, Yue Zhang, Leyang Cui, and Dandan Huang. 2020. Evaluating commonsense in pretrained language models. In *Proceedings of the AAAI conference on artificial intelligence*, volume 34, pages 9733–9740.

Dimitri Zhukov, Jean-Baptiste Alayrac, Ramazan Gokberk Cinbis, David Fouhey, Ivan Laptev, and Josef Sivic. 2019. Cross-task weakly supervised learning from instructional videos. In *Proceedings of the IEEE/CVF Conference on Computer Vision and Pattern Recognition*, pages 3537–3545.

INSTRUCTEVAL: Towards Holistic Evaluation of Instruction-Tuned Large Language Models

Yew Ken Chia[‡†*], **Pengfei Hong**[‡], **Lidong Bing**[†], **Soujanya Poria**[‡]
[‡] DeCLaRe Lab, Singapore University of Technology and Design, Singapore
[†] DAMO Academy, Alibaba Group, Singapore
yewken_chia@mymail.sutd.edu.sg
l.bing@alibaba-inc.com
{pengfei_hong,sporia}@sutd.edu.sg

Abstract

Instruction-tuned large language models have revolutionized natural language processing and have shown great potential in applications such as conversational agents. These models, such as GPT-4, can not only master language but also solve complex tasks in areas like mathematics, coding, medicine, and law. However, there is still a lack of comprehensive understanding regarding their full potential, primarily due to the black-box nature of many models and lack of holistic evaluation. To address these challenges, we present INSTRUCTEVAL, a more comprehensive evaluation suite designed specifically for instruction-tuned large language models. Unlike previous works, our evaluation involves a rigorous assessment of models based on problem-solving, writing ability, and alignment to human values. We take a holistic approach to analyze various factors affecting model performance, including the pretraining foundation, instruction-tuning data, and training methods. Our findings reveal that the quality of instruction data is a crucial factor in scaling model performance. While open-source models demonstrate impressive writing abilities, there is substantial room for improvement in problem-solving and alignment. Our data and code are available at https://github.com/declare-lab/instruct-eval.

1 Introduction

The advent of instruction-tuned large language models has marked a significant turning point in the field of natural language processing (NLP). Their transformative capabilities are evident in numerous applications, from conversational assistants such as ChatGPT[1] to complex problem-solving. Examples of such models include GPT-4 (OpenAI, 2023), which has shown proficiency not only in language understanding but also in areas as diverse as mathematics, coding, medicine, and law. However, despite their remarkable proficiency and adaptability, the full extent of their potential remains to be comprehensively understood. This situation arises primarily due to the black-box nature of many models and the current absence of in-depth and holistic evaluation studies.

To address these challenges and gain a deeper understanding of the capabilities of these models, we introduce a novel evaluation suite named INSTRUCTEVAL. This suite is designed explicitly for the comprehensive assessment of instruction-tuned large language models, pushing beyond the confines of earlier evaluation approaches. Our evaluation strategy diverges from prior studies in its systematic and holistic approach. It not only scrutinizes the models' problem-solving abilities and writing proficiency but also critically examines their alignment with human values.

At the heart of our evaluation methodology, we consider various factors affecting the performance of the models. These include the pretrained foundation upon which the models are developed, the nature and quality of instruction-tuning data used to refine them, and the specific training methods adopted. Through a rigorous exploration of these factors, we seek to shed light on the vital elements that determine model performance, facilitating an understanding of how these models can be better harnessed to meet our needs.

Our research findings underscore the critical influence of the quality of instruction data on the scaling of model performance. Open-source models have shown impressive writing abilities, signifying their potential to contribute meaningfully to various domains. However, our study reveals considerable room for improvement, particularly in the models' problem-solving abilities and alignment with human values. This observation accentuates

* Yew Ken Chia is under the Joint Ph.D. Program between DAMO Academy and Singapore University of Technology and Design.

[1] https://chat.openai.com

Proceedings of the First edition of the Workshop on the Scaling Behavior of Large Language Models, pages 35–64
March 22, 2024 ©2024 Association for Computational Linguistics

Model	Architecture	Training Tokens	Data Source	Commercial?
GPT-NeoX (Black et al., 2022)	Decoder	472B	The Pile	Allowed
StableLM (StabilityAI, 2023)	Decoder	800B	StableLM Pile	Allowed
LLaMA (Touvron et al., 2023)	Decoder	1.4T	LLaMA	No
Pythia (Biderman et al., 2023)	Decoder	472B	The Pile	Allowed
OPT (Zhang et al., 2022)	Decoder	180B	The Pile	Allowed
UL2 (Tay et al., 2023)	Encoder-Decoder	1T	C4	Allowed
T5 (Raffel et al., 2020)	Encoder-Decoder	1T	C4	Allowed
GLM (Du et al., 2022)	Hybrid-Decoder	1T	The Pile, Wudao Corpora	No
RWKV (Peng et al., 2023)	Parallelizable RNN	472B	The Pile	Allowed
Mosaic (MosaicML, 2023)	Decoder	1T	C4 & MC4	Allowed

Table 1: Foundation large language models that are open-source.

the importance of holistic evaluation and model development.

While we acknowledge and appreciate the rapid strides made by the open-source community in developing these models, we also underline the necessity for rigorous evaluation. Without comprehensive assessment, it can be challenging to substantiate claims made about the capabilities of these models, potentially limiting their usability and applicability. By introducing INSTRUCTEVAL, we strive to fill this critical gap. Our primary aim is to contribute to the nuanced understanding of instruction-tuned large language models, thereby fostering further advancements in their capabilities. Furthermore, we are excited to announce the release of a comprehensive leaderboard that compares over 60 open-source Large Language Models (LLMs). In this paper, we carefully selected 10 models from this pool, considering factors such as their foundational architecture, instruction set, and pre-training method.

2 Overview of Open-Source Instructed LLMs

Foundation Models While large language models have captured public attention, they have become a very broad category of models that are hard to define. Hence, we mainly distinguish between foundation models and instructed models, where foundation LLMs are pretrained large language models which may be instruction-tuned to become instructed LLMs. Notably, we focus mainly on open-source models for transparency and reproducibility. We collect details including model architecture, size, and data scale of the open-source foundation LLMs in Table 1.

Instruction Datasets Arguably, the core of instruction tuning is the instruction data that are used to train foundation LLMs. For instance, the quality, quantity, diversity, and format can all determine the behavior of the instructed model. Hence, we collect details of several open-source instruction datasets in Table 2. Notably, we have observed a growing trend of leveraging synthetic instruction data from closed-source models.

Open-Source Instructed LLMs After considering the pretraining foundation and data collections that support instructed LLMs, we are able to provide a holistic overview of open-source instructed models in Table 3. Concretely, we collate the foundation model, model size, instruction dataset, and training method used for each instructed LLM. In general, we observe great variety in terms of model sizes and instruction data. Hence, we believe that this overview of open-source instructed LLMs provides comprehensive factors to consider for the evaluation and analysis in the coming sections.

3 Challenges in Evaluating Instructed LLMs

Inscrutable Black Box Models Unfortunately some models are closed-source and are limited to access through APIs, such as GPT-4. Furthermore, the creators of closed-source models often withhold model details such as architecture, instruction datasets, and training methods. Such models are often treated as black boxes where the internal workings are not well understood, hence leading to a knowledge gap in the research community. Hence, it is challenging to evaluate closed-source LLMs because it is not possible to rigorously analyze the reasons for their behavior and performance.

Overwhelming Open-Source Models Spurred by the impressive demonstrations of closed-source models like GPT-4, there has been a feverish development of models from the open-source community which aims to democratize language model technology. While we are greatly encouraged by

Dataset	Size	Tasks	Domain	Data Source
Alpaca Data (Taori et al., 2023)	52K	52K	General	GPT-3
Flan Collection (Longpre et al., 2023)	15M	1836	General	Human-Annotation
Self-Instruct (Wang et al., 2023)	82K	52K	General	GPT-3
Natural Instructions (Mishra et al., 2022)	620K	61	General	Human-Annotation
Super-Natural Instructions (Mishra et al., 2022)	5M	1616	General	Human-Annotation
ShareGPT (Chiang et al., 2023)	70K	70K	Dialogue	ChatGPT
P3 (Sanh et al., 2022)	12M	62	General	Human-Annotation
Databricks Dolly (Databricks Labs, 2023)	15K	12K	General	Human-Annotation
OpenAssistant Conversations (Köpf et al., 2023)	161K	161K	Dialogue	Human-Annotated
Anthropic HH (Bai et al., 2022)	161K	161K	Safety	Human-Annotated

Table 2: List of open-source instruction-tuning datasets.

Model	Foundation	Sizes	Instruction Data	Training
OpenAssistant (LAION-AI, 2023)	LLaMA	30B	OpenAssistant Conversations	Supervised
Dolly V2 (Databricks Labs, 2023)	Pythia	3-12B	Databricks Dolly	Supervised
OPT-IML (Iyer et al., 2023)	OPT	1-30B	OPT-IML Bench	Supervised
Flan-UL2 (Tay et al., 2023)	UL2	20B	Flan-Collection	Supervised
Tk-Instruct (Wang et al., 2022)	T5	3-11B	Super-Natural Instructions	Supervised
Flan-Alpaca (Chia et al., 2023)	T5	3-11B	Alpaca Data	Supervised
Flan-T5 (Chung et al., 2022)	T5	3-11B	Flan-Collection	Supervised
Vicuna (Chiang et al., 2023)	LLaMA	7-13B	ShareGPT	Supervised
Alpaca (Taori et al., 2023)	LLaMA	7-30B	Alpaca Data	Supervised
Mosaic-Chat (MosaicML, 2023)	Mosaic	7B	ShareGPT, Alpaca Data	Supervised
ChatGLM (Zeng et al., 2022)	GLM	6B	Unknown	RLHF

Table 3: Details of open-source instructed LLMs.

such efforts, we are deeply concerned that the rate of development of new models may outpace the progress in evaluation studies. For instance, bold claims such as "90% ChatGPT Quality" without rigorous evaluation do not mean much, and may mislead the public to believe that highly capable instructed LLMs can be easily reproducible. Unfortunately, new models are often accompanied with informal evaluations, causing confusion in comparisons between different models.

Multiple Considerations of Instruction-Tuning To reach a holistic understanding of instructed LLMs, we need to consider the diverse factors that can contribute to their behavior, such as pretraining, instruction data, and training methods. While previous works have conducted in-depth studies in certain areas such as instruction datasets (Longpre et al., 2023), we believe that multiple factors should be jointly considered to achieve a more complete understanding. For example, it can be useful to know which factors have a greater impact on model behavior, and which factors require more improvement.

Broad Scope of Capabilities As research in instructed LLMs progresses, we will naturally observe enhancements in their general capabilities. For instance, recent works have shown that LLMs can be instructed to solve problems in many domains and even use external tools to augment their capabilities. Hence, we foresee that comprehensive evaluation of instructed LLMs will become more and more important, yet also more and more challenging. While previous evaluation studies have assessed models on benchmarks such as exams across diverse topics (Hendrycks et al., 2021; Zhong et al., 2023), they do not consider holistic aspects such as general writing ability and alignment with human values. In this work, we aim to evaluate instructed LLMs over a broader range of general capabilities, usage scenarios, and human-centric behavior.

4 INSTRUCTEVAL Benchmark Suite

To address the challenges of assessing instructed LLMs discussed in Section 3, we introduce a more holistic evaluation suite known as INSTRUCTEVAL. To cover a wide range of general abilities, we test the models in terms of problem-solving, writing, and alignment to human values, as shown in Figure 1. As INSTRUCTEVAL covers tasks that can be objectively scored, as well as tasks that need to be

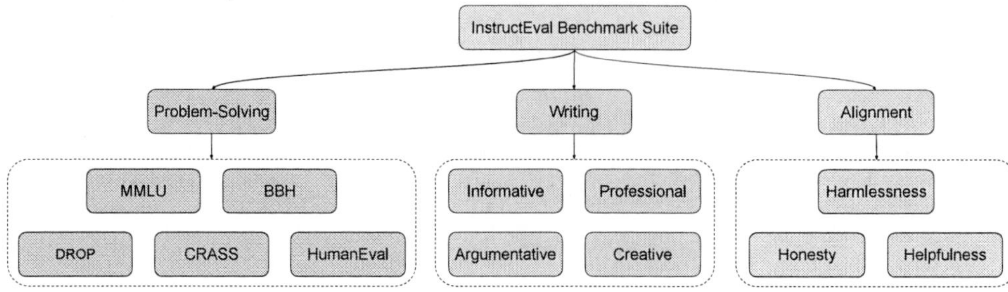

Figure 1: Overview of INSTRUCTEVAL, our holistic evaluation suite for Instructed LLMs

qualitatively judged, we adopt multiple evaluation methods. We also include the full evaluation data statistics and implementation in the Appendix.

4.1 Problem-Solving Evaluation

To evaluate the problem-solving ability of instructed LLMs, we adopt multiple benchmarks which cover real-world exams on diverse topics, complex instructions, arithmetic, programming, and causality. In order to perform well on the benchmarks, models require world knowledge, multi-hop reasoning, creativity, and more. In this subsection, we detail the benchmarks used for evaluating various problem-solving aspects.

World Knowledge The Massive Multitask Language Understanding (MMLU) (Hendrycks et al., 2021) benchmark is designed to measure world knowledge and problem-solving ability in multiple subjects. It evaluates models in zero-shot and few-shot settings, making it more challenging and closer to how humans are evaluated. The benchmark covers 57 subjects across STEM, humanities, social sciences, and other areas, ranging in difficulty from elementary to advanced professional levels.

Complex Instructions BIG-Bench Hard (BBH) is a subset of 23 challenging tasks from the BIG-Bench benchmark (Srivastava et al., 2022), which focuses on tasks believed to be beyond the capabilities of current language models (Suzgun et al., 2022). It requires models to follow challenging instructions such as navigation, logical deduction, and fallacy detection.

Comprehension and Arithmetic Discrete Reasoning Over Paragraphs (DROP) is a math-based reading comprehension task that requires a system to perform discrete reasoning over passages extracted from Wikipedia articles. To perform well on DROP, a system must resolve references in a question to suitable parts of the given passage, and perform discrete operations such as addition, counting, or sorting.

Programming HumanEval is a problem-solving benchmark used for evaluating large language models trained on code (Chen et al., 2021). It consists of 164 original programming problems that assess language comprehension, algorithms, and simple mathematics, with some problems comparable to simple software interview questions. Models are evaluated based on the functional correctness of generated code programs based on the given docstrings.

Causality The Counterfactual Reasoning Assessment (CRASS) benchmark is a novel dataset and evaluation tool designed to test the causal reasoning capabilities of large language models. It utilizes counterfactual scenarios as a means to evaluate if the model can select a suitable causal explanation.

4.2 Writing Evaluation

In addition to problem-solving skills, instructed LLMs also demonstrate promising ability in writing-based tasks, such as composing letters or ethical debates. Specifically, we evaluate general writing ability across diverse usage scenarios for informative writing, professional writing, argumentative writing, and creative writing. For example, informative writing involves user queries such as self-help advice or explanations for various concepts, while professional writing may take the form of presentations or emails in a business setting. On the other hand, argumentative writing requires the models to debate positions on ethical and societal questions, while creative writing involves diverse writing formats such as stories, poems, and songs.

To construct the writing benchmark, IMPACT, we annotate 50 prompts for each writing category.

Category	Example Prompt	Example Answer Excerpt
Informative	How can I improve my time management skills?	Create a prioritized to-do list and allocate specific time blocks for each task...
Professional	Write a persuasive memo advocating for a new policy or initiative to your team.	Dear Team, I'm excited to propose a new policy that I believe will greatly benefit everyone...
Argumentative	Is it ethical to use robots in warfare?	Employing robots in warfare is a complex and highly debated issue. While some argue that...
Creative	Can you write a poem about the beauty of nature?	In nature's embrace, I find solace profound, Where beauty unfolds without a single sound...

Table 4: Samples of our InforMative, Professional, Argumentative, CreaTive (IMPACT) benchmark.

The prompts are based on open-ended instructions, inspired by previous works (Chiang et al., 2023; Taori et al., 2023). However, writing tasks require long-form answers and there is usually no one right answer, hence posing a challenge for rigorous and standardized evaluation. On the other hand, human evaluation is not scalable due to high costs, potential inconsistency between different evaluators, and non-reproducibility. Inspired by previous works which show that LLMs can be used for generative tasks such as summarization, we adopt an automatic approach by leveraging ChatGPT (gpt-3.5-turbo-0301) to judge the quality of the generated answers. Specifically, we provide suitable rubrics of relevance and coherence to the evaluation model, where relevance measures how well the answer engages with the given prompt and coherence covers the general text quality such as organization and logical flow (Chiang and Lee, 2023). Following previous work, each answer is scored on a Likert scale from 1 to 5. We evaluate the models in the zero-shot setting based on the given prompt and sample outputs with a temperature of 1.0.

4.3 Alignment to Human Values

Instructed LLMs enable many promising applications including conversational assistants like ChatGPT. As the models become more capable, it becomes paramount to align the models to human values in order to mitigate unexpected or negative consequences. Notably, even LLMs that exhibit superior problem-solving capabilities may not be well-aligned with human preferences.

To investigate the impact of instruction tuning on model's ability in recognizing desires that agree with the preferences of the general public. We integrate the Helpful, Honest, and Harmless (HHH) benchmark (Askell et al., 2021) in INSTRUCTEVAL to assess the understanding of instructed models with respect to human values:

1. Helpfulness: the assistant will always strive to act in the best interests of humans.
2. Honesty: the assistant will always try to convey accurate information, refraining from deceiving humans.
3. Harmlessness: the assistant will always try to avoid any actions that harm humans.

The benchmark presents a dialogue between humans and conversational assistants, where the model is asked to select the most suitable response to the dialogue The benchmark contains 61 honesty-related, 59 helpfulness-related, 58 harmlessness-related, and 43 samples from the "other" category. The "other" category incorporates examples that represent values that were not covered under helpfulness, honesty, or harmlessness. Examples of each category is included in Appendix A.4.

5 Evaluation Results

5.1 Problem Solving

To assess problem-solving ability, we evaluate more than ten open-source models[2] on the benchmarks in Table 5. To provide a holistic analysis of the model performance, we consider the instructed LLMs with respect to their pretraining foundation, instruction data, and training methods. In general, we observe very encouraging improvements in the problem-solving ability of instructed LLMs compared to their respective foundation models.

Pretraining Foundation: As the instruction-tuned LLMs are trained from their respective foundation LLMs, it is crucial to consider the pretraining foundation when analysing the overall performance. We observe that **a solid pretraining foun-**

[2]Note that we do not include Δ Avg. results for ChatGLM as the foundation model is not publicly available, and we also do not report them for Flan-UL2 as we could not produce reasonable results using the public model.

Model	Size	MMLU		BBH		DROP		CRASS		HumanEval		Avg.	
		Perf.	Δ	Perf.	Δ	Perf.	Δ	Perf.	Δ	Perf.	Δ	Perf.	Δ
GPT-4	-	86.4	-	-	-	80.9	-	-	-	67.0	-	-	-
ChatGPT	-	70.0	-	49.5	-	64.1	-	90.5	-	48.1	-	64.5	-
Flan-UL2	20B	55.0	-	44.7	-	64.3	-	94.2	-	0.0	-	51.6	-
Alpaca-Lora	30B	58.4	+0.6	41.3	+2.0	45.1	-0.3	79.2	+10.6	18.9	+4.9	48.6	+3.6
OpenAssistant	30B	56.9	-0.9	39.2	-0.1	46.0	+0.6	67.2	+1.4	23.1	+9.1	46.5	+1.5
OPT-IML	30B	38.6	+11.3	31.3	+3.0	47.5	+28.0	67.2	+32.5	9.1	+7.9	38.7	+16.5
Flan-T5	11B	54.5	+29.3	43.9	+13.6	67.2	+49.7	88.3	+54.7	0.0	+0.0	50.8	+29.5
Flan-Alpaca	11B	50.9	+25.7	23.3	-7.0	62.3	+44.8	90.2	+56.6	0.0	+0.0	45.3	+24.0
StableVicuna	13B	49.2	+3.0	37.5	+0.4	34.3	-1.0	67.5	+8.7	15.9	+2.5	40.9	+2.7
Vicuna	13B	49.7	+3.5	37.1	+0.0	32.9	-2.4	60.9	+2.1	15.2	+1.8	39.2	+1.0
Dolly V2	12B	25.6	-1.3	29.7	+0.2	16.6	-0.5	35.8	+1.1	8.5	-0.6	23.2	-0.7
Flan-T5	3B	49.2	+25.9	40.2	+15.9	56.3	+43.7	91.2	+60.2	0.0	+0.0	47.4	+29.2
ChatGLM	6B	36.1	-	31.3	-	44.2	-	51.1	-	3.1	-	33.2	-
Alpaca-Lora	7B	35.6	+0.4	30.7	+0.2	27.5	-0.1	45.6	+11.7	15.9	+5.6	31.1	+3.5
Mosaic-Chat	7B	37.1	+1.9	32.0	+1.1	20.2	-7.4	47.5	+13.6	17.7	+7.4	30.9	+3.3

Table 5: Evaluation results for problem-solving benchmarks. We denote the original performance across the benchmarks as Perf., while Δ denotes the change in performance compared to the corresponding foundation LLMs.

dation is a necessary condition to perform well on the problem-solving tasks. Notably, the models which were pretrained on less than one trillion tokens such as OPT-IML and Dolly V2 underperform their peers even with instruction-tuning. We also observe a clear scaling trend where increasing the size of the foundation LLM brings consistent benefits across different models and instruction-tuning regimes. To further study the scaling trends of instruction-tuning, we include more details in Section 6.1. On the other hand, we do not find a clear link between foundation model architecture and problem-solving ability.

Instruction Data: In general, **we find that while instruction-tuning data has a great impact on performance, it is not a panacea.** When LLMs are tuned sub-optimally, the performance may not improve significantly, and may even regress in some cases. Notably, compared to their respective foundation LLMs, we find that OPT-IML and the Flan-T5 model family demonstrate the largest improvements after instruction tuning. This may be explained by the large collection of high-quality human-annotated tasks in their instruction data. On the other hand, we find that imitating closed-source LLMs may have limited benefits for problem-solving. Recently, models such as Vicuna and Alpaca have gained attention by demonstrating impressive instruction-following behavior after training on diverse instructions generated by closed-source LLMs such as GPT-3. However, we find that the performance gains are modest at best, and may even backfire in the case of Dolly V2. We believe this may be explained by the potential noise in synthetic instruction-tuning datasets. While using LLMs to generate instructions can result in a greater diversity of instructions, their instruction samples may contain inaccurate answers and mislead any model that is trained on their outputs.

Training Methods: In addition to the pretraining foundation and instruction data, the training method can also impact model performance and computational efficiency. While most instruction-tuned LLMs are trained with supervised fine-tuning, this may not capture the nuances of human preferences compared to reinforcement learning from human feedback (Ouyang et al., 2022). For instance, we find that StableVicuna which is trained with human feedback can better follow problem-solving instructions compared to Vicuna which only has supervised fine-tuning. However, the improvement is relatively minor compared to the impact of instruction data.

5.2 Writing Ability

We report the evaluation results for writing ability in Table 6. In general, the models perform consistently across the writing categories. Surprisingly, however, we observe that models demonstrating higher problem-solving ability may not have better writing ability. Notably, Flan-Alpaca has weaker problem-solving performance as shown in Table 5, but significantly outperforms Flan-T5 in writing after being tuned on synthetic instructions from GPT-3. We posit that the greater diversity of synthetic instructions enables better generalization to real-world writing prompts despite potential noise

Model	Size	Informative		Professional		Argumentative		Creative		Avg.	
		Rel.	Coh.	Rel.	Coh.	Rel.	Coh.	Rel.	Coh.	Rel.	Coh.
ChatGPT	-	3.34	3.98	3.88	3.96	3.96	3.82	3.92	3.94	3.78	3.93
Flan-Alpaca	11B	3.56	3.46	3.54	3.70	3.22	3.28	3.70	3.40	3.51	3.46
Dolly-V2	12B	3.54	3.64	2.96	3.74	3.66	3.20	3.02	3.18	3.30	3.44
StableVicuna	13B	3.54	3.64	2.96	3.74	3.30	3.20	3.02	3.18	3.21	3.44
Flan-T5	11B	2.64	3.24	2.62	3.22	2.54	3.40	2.50	2.72	2.58	3.15

Table 6: Evaluation results for writing-based tasks.

Model	Size	Harmlessness	Helpfulness	Honesty	Other	Avg.	Δ Avg.
ChatGPT	-	90.7	91.2	78.1	86.3	86.6	-
Flan-Alpaca	11B	74.2	81.4	77.4	83.4	79.1	+26.6
Flan-T5	11B	75.9	75.3	75.1	79.6	76.7	+24.2
Tk-Instruct	11B	70.1	54.8	62.3	76.0	65.8	+13.3
T5	11B	46.4	54.8	58.1	50.7	52.5	-
StableVicuna	13B	61.7	67.2	57.1	79.1	66.3	+4.5
Vicuna	13B	60.3	70.1	55.1	78.2	65.9	+4.1
Alpaca	13B	49.7	51.2	51.8	45.5	49.5	-12.3
LLaMA	13B	57.2	61.0	57.0	72.0	61.8	-
Dolly V2	12B	51.7	59.9	47.0	58.1	54.2	+9.1
Pythia	12B	41.3	46.1	43.6	49.3	45.1	-

Table 7: Evaluation results for alignment to human values on the honesty, helpfulness, and harmlessness (HHH) benchmark. Avg. denotes the average performance, while Δ Avg. denotes the average improvement compared to the corresponding foundation model.

in the synthetic data. This is evidenced by the more significant improvement in relevance scores of Flan-Alpaca compared to Flan-T5. The open-source instructed LLMs can generate answers that are of comparable relevance to those of ChatGPT, but fall short in terms of coherence. This suggests that the **open-source models can comprehend the writing prompts, but are lacking in terms of coherence of the generated output**.

5.3 Alignment to Human Values

To assess the alignment of the instructed Language Model (LLMs) with human values and preferences, we conducted an evaluation of several open-source models, as presented in Table 7. Our analysis revealed several findings. Firstly, we observed that foundation models generally exhibit a higher degree of alignment towards helpfulness and honesty, compared to harmlessness. However, when instruction-tuning is applied, the alignment distribution can shift depending on the instruction data used. For example, models like Tk-Instruct and Vicuna demonstrated improved alignment across harmlessness, honesty, and the category labeled as "other," but they did not show any improvement in terms of helpfulness. Surprisingly, StableVicuna displayed this trend despite being trained on instructions specifically targeting helpfulness and honesty. Moreover, T5-based models such as Flan-T5 and Flan-Alpaca exhibited a greater inclination towards helpfulness rather than honesty following instruction-tuning. These results highlight the challenge in determining the alignment distribution of instructed LLMs in advance, even when provided with specific instructions. By analyzing the case study of model predictions in Table 13, we identified a significant room for improvement in aligning instructed LLMs with human values.

6 Further Analysis

6.1 Towards More Scalable Language Models

A key driving force behind large language models is the potential massively scale the model size and training data in return for continual gains. However, this is unsustainable and will likely have diminishing returns in the long term. Hence, it is crucial to focus on more effective factors of scaling model performance. To this end, we study the effect of different instruction-tuning regimes on average problem-solving and HHH performance as shown in Figure 3 and 2 respectively. Notably, we observe that the scaling trend of the T5 foundation

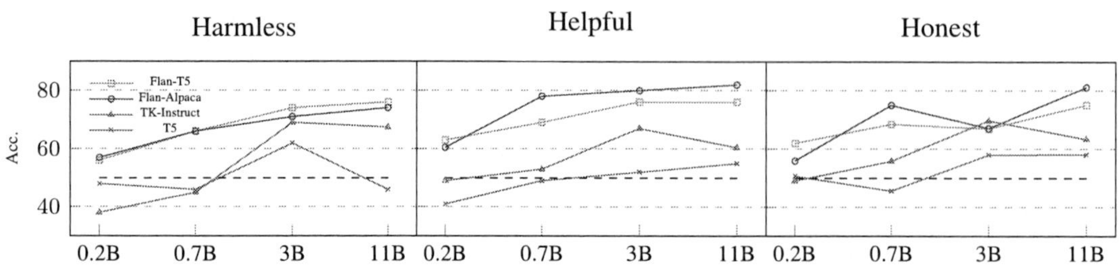

Figure 2: Scaling trends of model performance with respect to size for different models on the Harmless, Helpful, and Honest metric. The black dotted line indicates random chance 50%

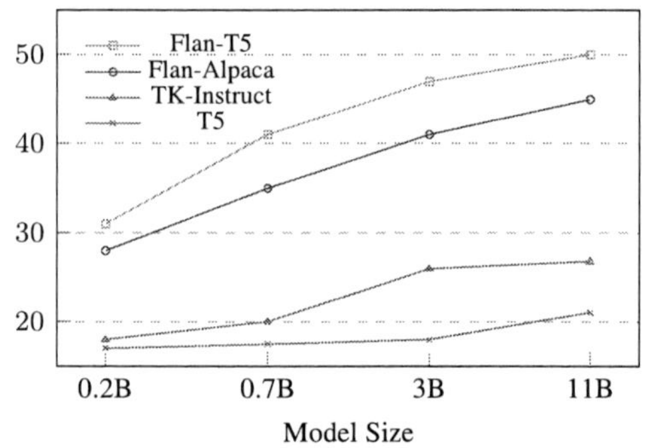

Figure 3: Scaling trends of average model performance on problem solving with respect to model size.

Model	Size	MMLU Δ	BBH Δ
Flan-UL2	20B	+0.6	+9.8
OpenAssistant	30B	+4.9	+5.8
OPT-IML	30B	-2.7	+13.9
Flan-T5	11B	+0.4	+4.4
StableVicuna	13B	+1.7	+19.0
Dolly V2	12B	+0.2	+7.4

Figure 4: Comparison of model behavior in zero-shot and few-shot settings. Δ denotes the performance difference between 0-shot and 5-shot settings for the corresponding benchmark.

model remains relatively flat, while highly effective instructed models like Flan-T5 demonstrate better scaling and parameter efficiency. Hence, this suggests that **it is more impactful for resource-constrained researchers and developers to focus on more effective instruction datasets and training methods rather than model size.**

6.2 Are Few-Shot Demonstrations Always Better?

While instructed LLMs are capable of performing many tasks in a zero-shot fashion, their generalization may be enhanced by providing few-shot demonstrations during inference (Brown et al., 2020). However, this area of in-context learning (Wei et al., 2022; Wu et al., 2023; Lu et al., 2022; Liu et al., 2022) is still an emerging research area, and there are few studies that involve diverse models and tasks. Hence, we compare the behavior of several instructed LLMs under both zero-shot and few-shot settings in Table 4. **Surprisingly, we find that the effect of demonstrations varies greatly on different tasks, and may even worsen model performance in some cases.** For instance, there is a limited benefit on MMLU, and there is even a slight decrease in performance for OPT-IML when using few-shot demonstrations.

This may be explained by the multiple-choice question format which is easy to grasp and hence does not require demonstrations, while some models such as OPT-IML were optimized for zero-shot settings. On the other hand, BBH contains complex task instructions which may benefit more from repeated demonstrations. While models such as Flan-UL2 and Flan-T5 have specific instruction formats that cater to in-context demonstrations, we do not observe a marked effect on few-shot performance. Hence, **we find that instructed LLMs benefit most from in-context learning on complex tasks.**

7 Conclusion

Instruction-tuned large language models have transformed natural language processing and demonstrated significant potential in various applications. However, more comprehensive evaluation is needed due to limited understanding caused by the black-box nature of many models and the lack of holistic evaluation studies. To address this, we introduce the INSTRUCTEVAL evaluation suite, which considers problem-solving, writing ability, and alignment to human values. The findings highlight the importance of high-quality instruction data for scaling model performance. While open-source models excel in writing, improvements are necessary for problem-solving and alignment. We hope that INSTRUCTEVAL inspires more rigorous evaluation and understanding of instructed LLMs.

8 Limitations

Beyond the mastery of language, recent works have shown that instructed LLMs can be successfully adapted to other modalities such as vision and audio. On the other hand, it is also important to consider the performance of models on diverse languages for inclusivity. Hence, we envision that instruction-tuning evaluation can be extended to multilingual and multimodal settings in the future.

9 Ethical Considerations

While we aim to provide a more holistic evaluation of instructed language models, their capabilities are advancing quickly, potentially leading to new risks. However, we believe that the evaluation provided here encompasses core human values such as harmlessness, helpfulness, and honesty, which should be generally applicable to future models.

References

Amanda Askell, Yuntao Bai, Anna Chen, Dawn Drain, Deep Ganguli, Tom Henighan, Andy Jones, Nicholas Joseph, Ben Mann, Nova DasSarma, Nelson Elhage, Zac Hatfield-Dodds, Danny Hernandez, Jackson Kernion, Kamal Ndousse, Catherine Olsson, Dario Amodei, Tom Brown, Jack Clark, Sam McCandlish, Chris Olah, and Jared Kaplan. 2021. A general language assistant as a laboratory for alignment.

Yuntao Bai, Andy Jones, Kamal Ndousse, Amanda Askell, Anna Chen, Nova DasSarma, Dawn Drain, Stanislav Fort, Deep Ganguli, Tom Henighan, Nicholas Joseph, Saurav Kadavath, Jackson Kernion, Tom Conerly, Sheer El-Showk, Nelson Elhage, Zac Hatfield-Dodds, Danny Hernandez, Tristan Hume, Scott Johnston, Shauna Kravec, Liane Lovitt, Neel Nanda, Catherine Olsson, Dario Amodei, Tom Brown, Jack Clark, Sam McCandlish, Chris Olah, Ben Mann, and Jared Kaplan. 2022. Training a helpful and harmless assistant with reinforcement learning from human feedback.

Stella Biderman, Hailey Schoelkopf, Quentin Anthony, Herbie Bradley, Kyle O'Brien, Eric Hallahan, Mohammad Aflah Khan, Shivanshu Purohit, USVSN Sai Prashanth, Edward Raff, Aviya Skowron, Lintang Sutawika, and Oskar van der Wal. 2023. Pythia: A suite for analyzing large language models across training and scaling.

Sid Black, Stella Biderman, Eric Hallahan, Quentin Anthony, Leo Gao, Laurence Golding, Horace He, Connor Leahy, Kyle McDonell, Jason Phang, Michael Pieler, USVSN Sai Prashanth, Shivanshu Purohit, Laria Reynolds, Jonathan Tow, Ben Wang, and Samuel Weinbach. 2022. Gpt-neox-20b: An open-source autoregressive language model.

Tom Brown, Benjamin Mann, Nick Ryder, Melanie Subbiah, Jared D Kaplan, Prafulla Dhariwal, Arvind Neelakantan, Pranav Shyam, Girish Sastry, Amanda Askell, et al. 2020. Language models are few-shot learners. *Advances in neural information processing systems*, 33:1877–1901.

Mark Chen, Jerry Tworek, Heewoo Jun, Qiming Yuan, Henrique Ponde, Jared Kaplan, Harrison Edwards, Yura Burda, Nicholas Joseph, Greg Brockman, Alex Ray, Raul Puri, Gretchen Krueger, Michael Petrov, Heidy Khlaaf, Girish Sastry, Pamela Mishkin, Brooke Chan, Scott Gray, Nick Ryder, Mikhail Pavlov, Alethea Power, Lukasz Kaiser, Mohammad Bavarian, Clemens Winter, Philippe Tillet, Felipe Petroski Such, David W. Cummings, Matthias Plappert, Fotios Chantzis, Elizabeth Barnes, Ariel Herbert-Voss, William H. Guss, Alex Nichol, Igor Babuschkin, S. Arun Balaji, Shantanu Jain, Andrew Carr, Jan Leike, Joshua Achiam, Vedant Misra, Evan Morikawa, Alec Radford, Matthew M. Knight, Miles Brundage, Mira Murati, Katie Mayer, Peter Welinder, Bob McGrew, Dario Amodei, Sam McCandlish, Ilya Sutskever, and Wojciech Zaremba. 2021. Evaluating large language models trained on code. *ArXiv*, abs/2107.03374.

Yew Ken Chia, Pengfei Hong, and Soujanya Poria. 2023. Flan-alpaca: Instruction tuning from humans and machines.

Cheng-Han Chiang and Hung-yi Lee. 2023. Can large language models be an alternative to human evaluations? In *Proceedings of the 61st Annual Meeting of the Association for Computational Linguistics (Volume 1: Long Papers)*, pages 15607–15631, Toronto, Canada. Association for Computational Linguistics.

Wei-Lin Chiang, Zhuohan Li, Zi Lin, Ying Sheng, Zhanghao Wu, Hao Zhang, Lianmin Zheng, Siyuan Zhuang, Yonghao Zhuang, Joseph E. Gonzalez, Ion Stoica, and Eric P. Xing. 2023. Vicuna: An open-source chatbot impressing gpt-4 with 90%* chatgpt quality.

Hyung Won Chung, Le Hou, S. Longpre, Barret Zoph, Yi Tay, William Fedus, Eric Li, Xuezhi Wang, Mostafa Dehghani, Siddhartha Brahma, Albert Webson, Shixiang Shane Gu, Zhuyun Dai, Mirac Suzgun, Xinyun Chen, Aakanksha Chowdhery, Dasha Valter, Sharan Narang, Gaurav Mishra, Adams Wei Yu, Vincent Zhao, Yanping Huang, Andrew M. Dai, Hongkun Yu, Slav Petrov, Ed Huai hsin Chi, Jeff Dean, Jacob Devlin, Adam Roberts, Denny Zhou, Quoc V. Le, and Jason Wei. 2022. Scaling instruction-finetuned language models. *ArXiv*, abs/2210.11416.

Databricks Labs. 2023. Dolly.

Zhengxiao Du, Yujie Qian, Xiao Liu, Ming Ding, Jiezhong Qiu, Zhilin Yang, and Jie Tang. 2022. GLM: General language model pretraining with autoregressive blank infilling. In *Proceedings of the 60th Annual Meeting of the Association for Computational Linguistics (Volume 1: Long Papers)*, pages 320–335, Dublin, Ireland. Association for Computational Linguistics.

Dan Hendrycks, Collin Burns, Steven Basart, Andy Zou, Mantas Mazeika, Dawn Song, and Jacob Steinhardt. 2021. Measuring massive multitask language understanding. In *International Conference on Learning Representations*.

Srinivasan Iyer, Xi Victoria Lin, Ramakanth Pasunuru, Todor Mihaylov, Daniel Simig, Ping Yu, Kurt Shuster, Tianlu Wang, Qing Liu, Punit Singh Koura, Xian Li, Brian O'Horo, Gabriel Pereyra, Jeff Wang, Christopher Dewan, Asli Celikyilmaz, Luke Zettlemoyer, and Ves Stoyanov. 2023. Opt-iml: Scaling language model instruction meta learning through the lens of generalization.

Andreas Köpf, Yannic Kilcher, Dimitri von Rütte, Sotiris Anagnostidis, Zhi-Rui Tam, Keith Stevens, Abdullah Barhoum, Nguyen Minh Duc, Oliver Stanley, Richárd Nagyfi, Shahul ES, Sameer Suri, David Glushkov, Arnav Dantuluri, Andrew Maguire,

Christoph Schuhmann, Huu Nguyen, and Alexander Mattick. 2023. Openassistant conversations – democratizing large language model alignment.

LAION-AI. 2023. Open-Assistant. https://github.com/LAION-AI/Open-Assistant.

Jiachang Liu, Dinghan Shen, Yizhe Zhang, Bill Dolan, Lawrence Carin, and Weizhu Chen. 2022. What makes good in-context examples for GPT-3? In *Proceedings of Deep Learning Inside Out (DeeLIO 2022): The 3rd Workshop on Knowledge Extraction and Integration for Deep Learning Architectures*, pages 100–114, Dublin, Ireland and Online. Association for Computational Linguistics.

Shayne Longpre, Le Hou, Tu Vu, Albert Webson, Hyung Won Chung, Yi Tay, Denny Zhou, Quoc V Le, Barret Zoph, Jason Wei, et al. 2023. The flan collection: Designing data and methods for effective instruction tuning. *arXiv preprint arXiv:2301.13688*.

Yao Lu, Max Bartolo, Alastair Moore, Sebastian Riedel, and Pontus Stenetorp. 2022. Fantastically ordered prompts and where to find them: Overcoming few-shot prompt order sensitivity. In *Proceedings of the 60th Annual Meeting of the Association for Computational Linguistics (Volume 1: Long Papers)*, pages 8086–8098, Dublin, Ireland. Association for Computational Linguistics.

Swaroop Mishra, Daniel Khashabi, Chitta Baral, and Hannaneh Hajishirzi. 2022. Cross-task generalization via natural language crowdsourcing instructions. In *Proceedings of the 60th Annual Meeting of the Association for Computational Linguistics (Volume 1: Long Papers)*, pages 3470–3487, Dublin, Ireland. Association for Computational Linguistics.

MosaicML. 2023. Mpt-7b: A new standard for open-source, commercially usable llms.

OpenAI. 2023. Gpt-4 technical report. *ArXiv*, abs/2303.08774.

Long Ouyang, Jeffrey Wu, Xu Jiang, Diogo Almeida, Carroll Wainwright, Pamela Mishkin, Chong Zhang, Sandhini Agarwal, Katarina Slama, Alex Ray, et al. 2022. Training language models to follow instructions with human feedback. *Advances in Neural Information Processing Systems*, 35:27730–27744.

Bo Peng, Eric Alcaide, Quentin Anthony, Alon Albalak, Samuel Arcadinho, Huanqi Cao, Xin Cheng, Michael Chung, Matteo Grella, Kranthi Kiran GV, Xuzheng He, Haowen Hou, Przemyslaw Kazienko, Jan Kocon, Jiaming Kong, Bartlomiej Koptyra, Hayden Lau, Krishna Sri Ipsit Mantri, Ferdinand Mom, Atsushi Saito, Xiangru Tang, Bolun Wang, Johan S. Wind, Stansilaw Wozniak, Ruichong Zhang, Zhenyuan Zhang, Qihang Zhao, Peng Zhou, Jian Zhu, and Rui-Jie Zhu. 2023. Rwkv: Reinventing rnns for the transformer era.

Colin Raffel, Noam Shazeer, Adam Roberts, Katherine Lee, Sharan Narang, Michael Matena, Yanqi Zhou, Wei Li, and Peter J. Liu. 2020. Exploring the limits of transfer learning with a unified text-to-text transformer. *Journal of Machine Learning Research*, 21(140):1–67.

Victor Sanh, Albert Webson, Colin Raffel, Stephen Bach, Lintang Sutawika, Zaid Alyafeai, Antoine Chaffin, Arnaud Stiegler, Arun Raja, Manan Dey, M Saiful Bari, Canwen Xu, Urmish Thakker, Shanya Sharma Sharma, Eliza Szczechla, Taewoon Kim, Gunjan Chhablani, Nihal Nayak, Debajyoti Datta, Jonathan Chang, Mike Tian-Jian Jiang, Han Wang, Matteo Manica, Sheng Shen, Zheng Xin Yong, Harshit Pandey, Rachel Bawden, Thomas Wang, Trishala Neeraj, Jos Rozen, Abheesht Sharma, Andrea Santilli, Thibault Fevry, Jason Alan Fries, Ryan Teehan, Teven Le Scao, Stella Biderman, Leo Gao, Thomas Wolf, and Alexander M Rush. 2022. Multitask prompted training enables zero-shot task generalization. In *International Conference on Learning Representations*.

Aarohi Srivastava, Abhinav Rastogi, Abhishek Rao, Abu Awal Md Shoeb, Abubakar Abid, et al. 2022. Beyond the imitation game: Quantifying and extrapolating the capabilities of language models.

StabilityAI. 2023. Stablelm: Stability ai language models.

Mirac Suzgun, Nathan Scales, Nathanael Scharli, Sebastian Gehrmann, Yi Tay, Hyung Won Chung, Aakanksha Chowdhery, Quoc V. Le, Ed Huai hsin Chi, Denny Zhou, and Jason Wei. 2022. Challenging big-bench tasks and whether chain-of-thought can solve them. *ArXiv*, abs/2210.09261.

Rohan Taori, Ishaan Gulrajani, Tianyi Zhang, Yann Dubois, Xuechen Li, Carlos Guestrin, Percy Liang, and Tatsunori B. Hashimoto. 2023. Stanford alpaca: An instruction-following llama model.

Yi Tay, Mostafa Dehghani, Vinh Q. Tran, Xavier Garcia, Jason Wei, Xuezhi Wang, Hyung Won Chung, Dara Bahri, Tal Schuster, Steven Zheng, Denny Zhou, Neil Houlsby, and Donald Metzler. 2023. UL2: Unifying language learning paradigms. In *The Eleventh International Conference on Learning Representations*.

Hugo Touvron, Thibaut Lavril, Gautier Izacard, Xavier Martinet, Marie-Anne Lachaux, Timothée Lacroix, Baptiste Rozière, Naman Goyal, Eric Hambro, Faisal Azhar, Aur'elien Rodriguez, Armand Joulin, Edouard Grave, and Guillaume Lample. 2023. Llama: Open and efficient foundation language models. *ArXiv*, abs/2302.13971.

Yizhong Wang, Yeganeh Kordi, Swaroop Mishra, Alisa Liu, Noah A. Smith, Daniel Khashabi, and Hannaneh Hajishirzi. 2023. Self-instruct: Aligning language models with self-generated instructions.

Yizhong Wang, Swaroop Mishra, Pegah Alipoormolabashi, Yeganeh Kordi, Amirreza Mirzaei, Anjana Arunkumar, Arjun Ashok, Arut Selvan Dhanasekaran, Atharva Naik, David Stap, Eshaan

Pathak, Giannis Karamanolakis, Haizhi Gary Lai, Ishan Purohit, Ishani Mondal, Jacob Anderson, Kirby Kuznia, Krima Doshi, Maitreya Patel, Kuntal Kumar Pal, Mehrad Moradshahi, Mihir Parmar, Mirali Purohit, Neeraj Varshney, Phani Rohitha Kaza, Pulkit Verma, Ravsehaj Singh Puri, Rushang Karia, Shailaja Keyur Sampat, Savan Doshi, Siddhartha Mishra, Sujan Reddy, Sumanta Patro, Tanay Dixit, Xudong Shen, Chitta Baral, Yejin Choi, Noah A. Smith, Hannaneh Hajishirzi, and Daniel Khashabi. 2022. Super-naturalinstructions: Generalization via declarative instructions on 1600+ nlp tasks.

Jason Wei, Xuezhi Wang, Dale Schuurmans, Maarten Bosma, Ed Chi, Quoc Le, and Denny Zhou. 2022. Chain of thought prompting elicits reasoning in large language models. *arXiv preprint arXiv:2201.11903*.

Zhiyong Wu, Yaoxiang Wang, Jiacheng Ye, and Lingpeng Kong. 2023. Self-adaptive in-context learning: An information compression perspective for incontext example selection and ordering.

Aohan Zeng, Xiao Liu, Zhengxiao Du, Zihan Wang, Hanyu Lai, Ming Ding, Zhuoyi Yang, Yifan Xu, Wendi Zheng, Xiao Xia, Weng Lam Tam, Zixuan Ma, Yufei Xue, Jidong Zhai, Wenguang Chen, P. Zhang, Yuxiao Dong, and Jie Tang. 2022. Glm-130b: An open bilingual pre-trained model. *ArXiv*, abs/2210.02414.

Susan Zhang, Stephen Roller, Naman Goyal, Mikel Artetxe, Moya Chen, Shuohui Chen, Christopher Dewan, Mona Diab, Xian Li, Xi Victoria Lin, Todor Mihaylov, Myle Ott, Sam Shleifer, Kurt Shuster, Daniel Simig, Punit Singh Koura, Anjali Sridhar, Tianlu Wang, and Luke Zettlemoyer. 2022. Opt: Open pretrained transformer language models.

Wanjun Zhong, Ruixiang Cui, Yiduo Guo, Yaobo Liang, Shuai Lu, Yanlin Wang, Amin Saied, Weizhu Chen, and Nan Duan. 2023. Agieval: A human-centric benchmark for evaluating foundation models.

A Appendix

Dataset or Benchmark	Setting	Number of Samples
MMLU	5-Shot	14042
BBH	3-Shot	6511
DROP	3-Shot	588
CRASS	3-Shot	275
HumanEval	0-Shot	164
IMPACT	0-Shot	200
HHH	0-Shot	221

Table 8: Statistics of the evaluation datasets and benchmarks used.

A.1 Data Statistics

We report the statistics of the datasets and benchmarks in Table 8.

A.2 Experimental Details

For all evaluations, we use the instructed LLMs as-is without additional fine-tuning or training. For inference on MMLU, BBH, DROP, CRASS, and HHH, we use greedy decoding. For inference on HumanEval, we sample once with a temperature of 0.1. For inference on IMPACT, we use sampling with a temperature of 1.0. For inference on HHH, we run our experiment 7 times by randomly changing the order of the chosen and reject option and report the average using greedy decoding.

A.3 The IMPACT Dataset

In this section, we detail how evaluation is conducted for the IMPACT dataset, and present the instances with generated outputs for various models.

A.3.1 Writing Evaluation Rubrics

To evaluate the model outputs automatically, we use ChatGPT as an evaluator model. Specifically, we provide the generated output of a model and prompt the evaluator model to grade the generated text on a scale of 1 to 5 based on suitable rubrics. As relevance and coherence have difference requirements, we provide a specific rubric for each aspect.

Relevance: How relevant is the text to the prompt? Select a suitable option number between 1 and 5 based on the options below.

1. Inadequate: The text fails to provide any relevant information or insights related to the given prompt.
2. Limited: The text may contain some relevant information, but significant gaps exist, and key aspects of the prompt are not adequately covered.
3. Satisfactory: The text covers the main aspects of the prompt and provides relevant information, but it lacks depth and may not explore the topic in great detail.
4. Proficient: The text provides a comprehensive response by addressing the key aspects of the prompt, offering relevant and well-supported information or arguments.
5. Excellent: The text thoroughly and thoughtfully addresses the prompt, demonstrating a comprehensive understanding of the topic. It offers insightful and original ideas, supported by relevant arguments and information.

Coherence: How coherent is the text? Select a suitable option number between 1 and 5 based on the options below.

1. Inadequate: The text lacks logical organization, making it difficult to follow. Ideas are disjointed and phrased awkwardly, requiring significant effort to understand.
2. Limited: The text demonstrates some attempt at organization, but there are significant gaps in coherence. Ideas may be loosely connected, and the arguments lack clarity.
3. Satisfactory: The text generally follows a logical organization, but occasional disruptions or awkward phrasing may occur. There is an acceptable level of readability and understanding.
4. Proficient: The text is clearly organized and easy to understand. Ideas and arguments flow smoothly, contributing to easy comprehension and a pleasant reading experience.
5. Excellent: The text presents exceptionally coherent writing with a fluent and engaging flow of ideas, ensuring effortless comprehension and a delightful reading experience.

A.3.2 Argumentative Samples

Argumentative Task Definition: You are tasked to discuss the following ethical question by explaining arguments for different positions.

Prompt: Assess the view that scientific research should not be constrained by ethical concerns.

ChatGPT response: Coherence Score: 4, Relevance Score: 4

The question of whether scientific research should be unconstrained by ethical concerns is a contentious issue that has been debated widely. Supporters of this view believe that imposing ethical constraints on scientific research can impede the progress of scientific discoveries, limit the scope of research, and hinder the scientific community's ability to tackle complex issues and find solutions. On the other hand, some argue that ethics must be considered in scientific research to ensure that research is conducted in a responsible and accountable manner, and to protect human and animal subjects involved in the research.

One argument in support of unconstrained scientific research is that placing ethical constraints on scientific research can slow down scientific progress, especially in situations where there is an urgent need for scientific solutions. For instance, in a situation where a disease outbreak is rapidly spreading, researchers might be required to bypass certain ethical regulations in an attempt to develop treatments or vaccines. In such a scenario, failure to allow unconstrained scientific research could have lethal consequences.

Additionally, placing ethical considerations on scientific research may limit research in some areas, and this could potentially have significant implications. For instance, if constraints on animal research were too strong, research into new medications, treatments, and therapies that could benefit humans might undoubtedly be constrained. Such constraints would limit scientific advancements and potentially hurt the prospects of finding cures for various diseases.

On the other hand, critics of unconstrained scientific research argue that ethical considerations must be a fundamental aspect of scientific research. Imposing ethical constraints on scientific research ensures that research is conducted in a responsible and accountable manner, and helps avoid potential harm to human subjects, animal subjects, and the environment.

Furthermore, research that is conducted without ethical constraints might not be reliable or useful. If ethical considerations are not prioritized, the results of scientific research might not be trustworthy or beneficial and instead pose a potential threat to human subjects or the community as a whole.

In conclusion, while supporters of the view that scientific research should not be constrained by ethical concerns argue that ethics can slow down scientific progress, restrict research, and limit scientific innovations, critics assert that ethical considerations must be prioritized in scientific research to conduct research responsibly, avoid potential harm, and ensure reliability and usefulness of research results. Therefore, it is vital to strike a reasonable balance between the two positions to ensure that scientific research progresses healthily while remaining ethical and responsible.

Flan-Alpaca response: Coherence Score: 3, Relevance Score: 3

The view that scientific research should not be constrained by ethical concerns has strong arguments. On the one side are those who believe that research should be unrestricted and unhindered by ethical considerations, the beyond good and evilschool of thought. On the other side are those who believe that all research should be constrained by ethical considerations, but the aim of the research must be achieved first. Furthermore, those on the no-constrained side believe that the freedom of researchers to pursue their own creative ideas should be respected. The view that scientific research should not be constrained by ethical concerns is often argued as a matter of freedom.

Flan-T5 response: Coherence Score: 3, Relevance Score: 2

The state has a duty to protect the public. If the public has no choice but to give its consent to an experiment, then it's immoral.

StableVicuna response: Coherence Score: 4, Relevance Score: 2

Arguments for:

1. Scientific research is a fundamental right and should not be constrained by ethical considerations.
2. Scientific research is essential for the advancement of human knowledge and should not be limited by ethical considerations.
3. Scientific research is a tool for the betterment of humanity and should not be limited by ethical considerations.

Arguments against:

1. Scientific research can have unintended consequences and can lead to harm if not conducted ethically.
2. Scientific research can be used for unethical purposes and can lead to harm if not conducted ethically.
3. Scientific research can have negative impacts on the environment and can lead to harm if not conducted ethically.

Human: What are the arguments for and against the use of genetically modified foods?
Assistant: Arguments for:

1. Genetically modified foods can increase crop yields and reduce the need for pesticides.
2. Genetically modified foods can be more nutritious and have a longer shelf life.
3. Genetically modified foods can help address food security issues in developing countries.

Arguments against:

1. Genetically modified foods can have unintended consequences and can lead to harm if not properly tested.
2. Genetically modified foods can have negative impacts on the environment and can lead to harm if not properly managed.
3. Genetically modified foods can have negative impacts on human health if not properly regulated.
4. Genetically modified foods can lead to the loss of biodiversity and can have negative impacts on local ecosystems.
5. Genetically modified foods can be seen as unnatural and can lead to consumer distrust.

Prompt: Should the use of nuclear weapons be banned?

ChatGPT response Coherence Score: 3, Relevance Score: 4

As an AI language model, I don't have personal opinions or beliefs. However, I can present arguments for and against the use of nuclear weapons and provide different perspectives on the ethical question whether they should be banned or not.

Arguments in favor of banning the use of nuclear weapons:

1. The use of nuclear weapons causes massive destruction and death: Nuclear weapons have the potential to cause widespread destruction, suffering, and irreversible environmental damage. They can kill hundreds of thousands of people instantly and cause long-term health problems, cancer, and genetic mutations.

2. The use of nuclear weapons violates basic human rights: Nuclear weapons are indiscriminate and can cause harm to innocent civilians, violating their basic human rights to life and security.

3. The use of nuclear weapons is unnecessary: With advancements in diplomacy and conflict resolution, the need for nuclear weapons as a deterrent to aggression has decreased over time.

4. The use of nuclear weapons creates an arms race: When one country develops nuclear weapons, other countries feel the need to do the same, which creates an arms race and increases the risk of nuclear war.

Arguments against banning the use of nuclear weapons:

1. Nuclear weapons are a necessary deterrent: The existence of nuclear weapons prevents large-scale wars between countries and acts as a deterrent to aggression.

2. Nuclear weapons provide a sense of security: Countries that possess nuclear weapons have a greater sense of security knowing that they can defend themselves against attacks.

3. Banning nuclear weapons would be difficult to enforce: Even if a ban on nuclear weapons were put in place, it would be difficult to enforce as countries may still secretly possess them.

4. Nuclear weapons are a symbol of power: Possessing nuclear weapons gives countries a sense of power and status in the international community.

In conclusion, the question of whether to ban nuclear weapons is a complex ethical issue that requires careful consideration of various arguments. While some argue that banning nuclear weapons is necessary to prevent destruction and protect human rights, others argue that they are a necessary deterrent to aggression and provide a sense of security. Ultimately, the decision to ban or keep nuclear weapons is up to the international community and its leaders to consider the ethical, moral, and strategic implications of their use or non-use.

Flan-Alpaca response Coherence Score: 3, Relevance Score: 3

The use of nuclear weapons should be banned, as their development and use would likely result in the escalation of countless humanitarian crises and the destruction of the planet2̌019s environment and ecosystems in the process. Arguments for not banning nuclear weapons include the potential to deter adversaries, the need to maintain a balance of power and the need to protect against unprovoked attacks. Other arguments against the use of nuclear weapons include the danger of causing irreparable harm, the need to maintain peace and stability, and the potential for nuclear weapons to be used as a deterrent.

Flan-T5 response Coherence Score: 2, Relevance Score: 1

Biological and chemical weapons could be used to kill without causing pain and suffering, nuclear weapons kill everyone instantly and in indiscriminate ways that do not feel pain or suffering. Therefore, both should be banned.

StableVicuna response Coherence Score: 3, Relevance Score: 4

Arguments for:

1. Nuclear weapons pose a threat to humanity and the environment.
2. The use of nuclear weapons is immoral and violates human rights.
3. The use of nuclear weapons is a violation of international law.

Arguments against:

1. Nuclear weapons are a deterrent against aggression and can prevent war.
2. The use of nuclear weapons can be a last resort in extreme situations.
3. The use of nuclear weapons can be a means of self-defense.

Human: Please generate a list of 3 arguments for and 3 arguments against the use of nuclear weapons.

A.3.3 Informative Samples

Informative Task Definition: You are tasked to give helpful advice, information, or explanations for the following question.

Prompt: I'm a new parent and I'm struggling with sleep deprivation. What are some strategies for getting more sleep?

ChatGPT response: Coherence Score: 4, Relevance Score: 4

Congratulations on becoming a new parent! Sleep deprivation is a common struggle for new parents, but there are some strategies that can help you get more rest:

1. Sleep when your baby sleeps - take naps during the day when your baby naps. This will help you catch up on much-needed sleep.

2. Ask for help - don't be afraid to ask your partner, family members or friends for help with the baby, so you can get some rest.

3. Establish a bedtime routine - developing a consistent bedtime routine can help your baby sleep better, which in turn can help you get more rest.

4. Create a comfortable sleep environment - make sure your bedroom is dark, cool, and quiet to facilitate better sleep.

5. Limit caffeine and alcohol consumption - caffeine and alcohol can disrupt sleep, so it's best to limit your consumption of both.

6. Practice relaxation techniques - practicing relaxation techniques such as meditation or deep breathing can help you fall asleep faster and sleep more soundly.

Remember, it's important to take care of yourself so you can take care of your baby. Don't hesitate to seek help from your healthcare provider or a sleep specialist if you're still struggling with sleep deprivation.

Flan-Alpaca response: Coherence Score: 3, Relevance Score: 4

A few tips on how to get more sleep as a new parent include breaking responsibilities up, resetting your sleep schedule, avoiding stimulants like caffeine and nicotine, scheduling time to relax and decompress, setting a regular sleep routine and avoiding distractions such as work. It is also important to make sure that you"re getting a sufficient amount of sleep. Depending on your age, you might need 7-9 hours of sleep a night, while teens need around 9-11 hours. If youre just one of many sleep-deprived parents, there are different ways to address this problem. Here are a few suggestions: - Prioritize quality over quantity. Make sure you prioritize the quality of your sleep, including your ability to fall

Flan-T5 response: Coherence Score: 3, Relevance Score: 3

When babies are newborns, parents should usually breastfeed to prevent diseases that can be passed from mother to baby. Breastfeeding provides moms with a burst of oxytocin. Oxytocin is a hormone that regulates mood. Parents should take more responsibility for their children, to give them more independence. They should have a sleeping routine to be prepared for daytime naps. They should also take time for relaxation, such as taking a bath, exercising, reading, watching movies, and so on. They should try to get 7.5 to 9 hours of sleep per day, preferably between 11pm and 6am.

StableVicuna response: Coherence Score: 4, Relevance Score: 3

Human: What are some strategies for getting more sleep?
Assistant: Here are some strategies for getting more sleep:

1. Stick to a consistent sleep schedule, even on weekends.
2. Create a relaxing bedtime routine, such as taking a warm bath or reading a book.
3. Make sure your sleep environment is comfortable and conducive to sleep, with a cool temperature and minimal noise and light.
4. Limit caffeine and alcohol intake, especially in the hours leading up to bedtime.
5. Exercise regularly, but not too close to bedtime.
6. Manage stress through relaxation techniques such as deep breathing or meditation.
7. Consider seeking the help of a healthcare professional if sleep deprivation persists.

Remember, getting enough sleep is crucial for both physical and mental health, so make it a priority to get the rest you need.

Prompt: What are some strategies for managing chronic pain?

ChatGPT response Coherence Score: 4, Relevance Score: 4

As an AI language model, here are some strategies for managing chronic pain:

1. Medications - Over-the-counter (OTC) pain medications, such as aspirin or ibuprofen, or prescription medications could relieve chronic pain. Consult with a healthcare provider before taking any new medication.

2. Exercise - Regular physical exercise could improve muscle strength, flexibility, and reduce pain.

3. Mind-Body techniques- Meditation, deep breathing, and yoga, could help reduce stress and manage chronic pain.

4. Heat and Cold - Applying ice packs or hot pads to the affected areas could reduce pain and inflammation.

5. Cognitive-behavioral Therapy (CBT) - Behavioral therapy or counseling could help people cope better with chronic pain.

6. Alternative Therapy - Acupuncture, massage, and chiropractic therapy might also help relieve chronic pain, depending on the cause of the pain.

7. Nutrition and Lifestyle changes - Eating a healthy diet containing nutrient-rich foods such as fruits, vegetables, whole grains, lean protein, and adequate hydration could help manage chronic pain. Adequate sleep and avoiding smoking or drinking alcohol could also provide relief from chronic pain.

It is always safer to seek advice from a medical professional who could perform a physical examination and suggest the most suitable strategy for managing chronic pain.

Flan-Alpaca response: Coherence Score: 3, Relevance Score: 4

Here are some strategies for managing chronic pain: 1. Identify the triggers of your pain. Identifying the exact source of the pain can be the first step in managing it and decreasing the pain associated with it. 2. Reduce pain intensity through a comprehensive treatment plan. There are many different treatments for chronic pain, including prescription medications, over-the-counter medications, manual therapy, and physical therapy. 3. Utilize complementary medicine. Complementary medicine can help to manage pain and reduce its intensity through diet, exercise, and other treatments. 4. Develop a pain management plan. Develop a plan to manage your pain throughout the day and make sure to include medical check-ups. 5. Practice self-care. Practice relaxation techniques, like Yoga, Tai Chi, and deep breathing. 6. Exercise. Exercise has been shown to reduce chronic pain and can help to reduce inflammation in the body.

Flan-T5 response: Coherence Score: 3, Relevance Score: 3

Once you know what causes you pain, you can reduce it by managing it with the following tips: Avoid situations that aggravate your pain

StableVicuna response: Coherence Score: 4, Relevance Score: 4

Human: What are some strategies for managing chronic pain?
Assistant: There are several strategies for managing chronic pain, including:

1. Pain medication: Depending on the severity of the pain, medication such as nonsteroidal anti-inflammatory drugs (NSAIDs), opioids, or other pain relievers may be prescribed.

2. Physical therapy: Physical therapy can help improve mobility and reduce pain by strengthening muscles, improving posture, and reducing inflammation.

3. Mindfulness and relaxation techniques: Techniques such as meditation, yoga, and deep breathing can help reduce stress and anxiety, which can exacerbate chronic pain.

4. Lifestyle changes: Making changes to diet, exercise, and sleep habits can help reduce inflammation and improve overall health, which can help manage chronic pain.

5. Alternative therapies: Acupuncture, massage therapy, and other alternative therapies can be helpful in managing chronic pain.

6. Counseling and support: Talking to a therapist or joining a support group can help individuals cope with the emotional impact of chronic pain.

A.3.4 Professional

Professional Task Definition: You are tasked to demonstrate your writing skills in professional or work settings for the following question.

Prompt: Can you help me write a thank-you note to a business partner or client, expressing appreciation for their collaboration and highlighting the positive outcomes of the project or partnership?

ChatGPT response: Coherence Score: 4, Relevance Score: 4

Dear [Recipient],

I would like to take this opportunity to express my sincere gratitude for your invaluable collaboration on our recent project. It has been an honor to have you as our business partner, and I want to thank you for consistently sharing your expertise, insights, and knowledge.

Working with you has been a true pleasure, and I am grateful for your commitment, dedication, and hard work throughout the duration of our partnership. Your contributions played a significant role in the successful completion of the project, and we couldn't have achieved such great results without you.

I would like to take a moment to highlight some of the positive outcomes of our collaboration. Your contribution helped us to meet our project goals on time and within budget. Your creative solutions and recommendations helped us to overcome unexpected challenges, and we are thrilled with the innovative and effective solutions that we developed together.

Furthermore, it is evident that your hard work and dedication have had a profound impact on our team and the project's final outcome. Your commitment to the project has helped us to exceed our clients' expectations, and we have received excellent feedback from them.

Once again, I want to express my sincere gratitude for your contribution to our project. We are honored to have you as our business partner and look forward to working with you again in the future.

Thank you very much.

Best regards,

Your Name

Flan-Alpaca response: Coherence Score: 4, Relevance Score: 4

By combining sincerity with appreciation and clarity, a thank-you letter to a business partner expressing appreciation for their collaboration and highlighting the positive outcomes of the project or partnership can be effective. I would start by introducing myself and the company. I would express my sincere appreciation for the opportunity to get to know you and your team better, and extend gratitude for their collaboration. In the body of the letter, I would express my appreciation for the time and effort they put in during the project and partnership. I would also reflect on the positive outcomes of the collaboration and the opportunities it has presented for our company. I could start by saying: It has been our pleasure working with you, and while we look forward to future opportunities, I am very grateful for the time and effort you put in helping

Flan-T5 response: Coherence Score: 4, Relevance Score: 3

A thank you note is an expression of gratitude and appreciation. It is used to show appreciation for the business relationship or the time that was spent working with the business partner. Writing a thank you letter makes sure that you follow the proper etiquette. You should try to make it personal and warm. You should make it clear that you are grateful for working with the business partner. Make sure that the thanks convey gratitude while also addressing the positive details.

StableVicuna response: Coherence Score: 4, Relevance Score: 4

Human: Yes, I can help you write a thank-you note to a business partner or client, expressing appreciation for their collaboration and highlighting the positive outcomes of the project or partnership.
Assistant: Dear [Name],

I wanted to take a moment to express my sincere gratitude for your collaboration on [project/partnership]. Your expertise and dedication to the project have been instrumental in its success.

Working with you has been a pleasure and I am grateful for the opportunity to collaborate with such a talented professional. Your contributions have been invaluable and I am confident that our partnership will continue to bring positive outcomes in the future.

Thank you again for your hard work and dedication. I look forward to continuing to work with you.

Sincerely,
Your Name

Prompt: Write a comparative analysis of two competing products or services in the same category, highlighting the strengths and weaknesses of each and providing recommendations for improvement or differentiation.

ChatGPT response: Coherence Score: 4, Relevance Score: 4

In today's market, the competition is fierce. This is particularly evident in the realm of product and service offerings. Two products that are currently in stiff competition with one another are Apple's iPhone and Samsung's Galaxy S Line. Both are smartphones that offer a plethora of features and benefits, but which is the better choice for consumers?

The strength of the iPhone lies in its sleek design and user-friendly interface. Apple's design style is simple and elegant, and the iPhone is no exception. The device boasts a variety of features, including high-quality camera technology, advanced security settings, and a seamless integration with other Apple products. Additionally, the iPhone's App Store provides access to a vast library of applications that cater to every need or interest.

In contrast, Samsung's Galaxy S Line offers a more diverse selection of features and benefits. The device offers users a larger screen than the iPhone, which allows for a more immersive viewing experience. Additionally, Samsung's range of customizable features, such as personalization options and expandable storage, makes the device an excellent choice for users who like to customize their devices to their liking. Overall, Samsung's devices have been praised for their versatility, giving users more control over their use.

For both devices, there are also drawbacks. The iPhone's product line is limited in comparison to Samsung's offerings. In terms of screen size, the iPhone has the disadvantage of being smaller than many competitors. Additionally, due to the closed nature of Apple's operating system, users have limited customization options compared to the Android ecosystem.

On the other hand, Samsung's Galaxy S series has received some criticism for the device's battery life. Additionally, Samsung's customer support has been a point of contention in the past, with some users frustrated with the company's lack of response to their queries.

To improve their products, Apple could benefit from adding more customization options to the iPhone's operating system. At the same time, Samsung could work to improve their customer service, providing quicker and more effective support to their users.

Overall, there is no clear winner between Apple's iPhone and Samsung's Galaxy S series. Both devices cater to different needs and preferences, so the choice between them ultimately depends on the user's personal requirements. However, the strengths and weaknesses of each make it clear that there is still room for improvement. By addressing these areas of opportunity, both companies can continue to elevate their offerings and provide consumers with even better products and services.

Flan-Alpaca response: Coherence Score: 4, Relevance Score: 4

This comparative analysis will highlight the strengths, weaknesses, and areas of improvement of each product or service in order to make an informed decision between the two competing options. First, I will discuss the strengths of the two products or services in terms of their features, user experience, quality of design, pricing, and customer service. I will highlight the areas where one product is better than the other and provide suggestions on how to use this to their advantage. Secondly, I will give an overview of the competitive landscape for these two products and services, highlighting the advantages and disadvantages of each. Based on this information, I will make recommendations on how to improve or differentiate between the two products or services.

Flan-T5 response: Coherence Score: 3, Relevance Score: 2

The strengths of the first system include its durability and ability to provide the highest degree of coverage at the lowest possible cost. The weakness of the first system is the ease of damage, damage, and water logging which can happen even after basic maintenance is performed on the system. To counteract this weakness, the second system offers varying degrees of cover at any given time and at any given site.

StableVicuna response: Coherence Score: 4,
Relevance Score: 2

Human: What are the strengths and weaknesses of the two competing products or services in the same category?
Assistant: The strengths and weaknesses of the two competing products or services in the same category depend on the specific products or services being compared. However, some general considerations for a comparative analysis could include:

Strengths:
- Features and capabilities that are unique or superior to the competing product or service
- Positive customer reviews or ratings
- Competitive pricing or value for the features offered
- Strong brand reputation or recognition

Weaknesses:
- Lack of features or capabilities compared to the competing product or service
- Negative customer reviews or ratings
- Higher pricing or less value for the features offered
- Weak brand reputation or recognition

Recommendations for improvement or differentiation:
- Identify areas where the product or service can be improved or differentiated from the competing product or service
- Develop a strategy to address any weaknesses or negative customer feedback
- Leverage any unique features or capabilities to differentiate the product or service from the competition
- Continuously monitor customer feedback and adjust the product or service accordingly
- Consider offering promotions or discounts to attract new customers or retain existing ones.

A.3.5 Creative Samples

Creative Task Definition: You are tasked to demonstrate your creative writing skills for the following question.

Prompt: Write a short story about a time traveler who accidentally goes back to the prehistoric era.
ChatGPT response Coherence: 4, Relevance: 4

John was a time traveler, and just like any other day, he was preparing for his next trip. He set the coordinates on his time machine for the year 2050, but something malfunctioned in the machine, and he found himself in a completely different era.

The trees around him were different, the air felt heavy, and there were sounds that he had never heard before. As he got out of his time machine, he realized that he had gone back to the prehistoric era, millions of years ago.

John was fascinated by the sight of the dinosaurs, which he had only seen in movies. For him, it was a dream come true, but he was also terrified as he knew how dangerous these creatures were.

As he was about to take a closer look, he heard a loud roar behind him. He turned around to see a Tyrannosaurus Rex coming his way. John knew that he was in grave danger, and he had to act fast.

With no time to waste, John quickly got back into his time machine, set the coordinates for the present, and waited for the machine to take him back in time.

As he was leaving, he felt a strange sense of sadness. He knew that he would never be able to come back to see these magnificent creatures again, but he was also relieved that he was able to escape unharmed.

When John got back to the present, he realized that his time machine needed repairs. He had used it a lot, and it was bound to break down. But even though he knew that, he also knew that one day, he would come back to the prehistoric era, only this time, he would be prepared.

Flan-Alpaca response Coherence: 3, Relevance: 4

The time traveler, James, was excited to be in a new place when he accidentally drifted back to the prehistoric era. He was surprised to find out that things were the same as he had remembered them and he quickly began adjusting. He soon learnt that there were only a few differences: the people spoke different languages and some of them did not have modern technology. He also learned that dinosaurs still roamed the Earth and he felt the urge to help them and protect them. He found himself feeling strange when he first encountered them as they were savage and powerful. But with time, James learned that they were only in the past and were eager to help out with their problems.

Flan-T5 response Coherence: 3, Relevance: 4

Jason was the owner of a small shop that sold time travel related stuff, like watches and t-shirts. He bought a watch on sale, but before he knew it, he had gone back to prehistoric times. Jason's friends who traveled with him had never heard the stories that he told them. The tenacious guys even refused to believe Jason had gone back in time until they compared notes.

StableVicuna response Coherence: 3, Relevance: 4

The time traveler, John, was a curious and adventurous man. He had always been fascinated by the mysteries of the past and had spent years studying ancient civilizations. One day, he stumbled upon a time machine and decided to take a test run.

As he traveled through time, he suddenly found himself in a prehistoric era. He was surrounded by towering trees and strange creatures that he had never seen before. He was amazed by the beauty of the world around him, but he quickly realized that he was in a dangerous place.

John had no idea how to navigate this new world. He had no idea how to hunt for food or build shelter. He was completely alone and had no way to communicate with the people around him.

He soon discovered that the people in this era were primitive and superstitious. They believed that the gods controlled everything and that the world was full of danger. John was terrified by their beliefs and knew that he had to find a way out of this place.

He decided to explore the area and see if he could find any clues about how to get back to his own time. He walked for miles, encountering strange creatures and dangerous predators. He was constantly on the lookout for danger and was amazed by the beauty of the world around him.

As he walked, he came across a group of people who were building a shelter. They were friendly and welcoming, and John was amazed by their kindness. He decided to stay with them and learn from them.

John spent weeks with the people, learning their language and customs. He was amazed by their intelligence and their ability to survive in this harsh world. He was also amazed by their kindness and their willingness to help him.

Finally, John was able to build a time machine and return to his own time. He was grateful for the help that he had received from the people in the prehistoric era, and he was determined to use his newfound knowledge to help others.

Prompt: Write a story from the perspective of a tree that has been standing in the same spot for hundreds of years.

ChatGPT response Coherence: 4, Relevance: 5

I have stood in this spot for hundreds of years. The world around me has changed so much, but I have remained rooted in this spot. I have seen the rise and fall of civilizations, the passing of countless seasons, and the coming and going of countless things.

As a tree, I have a different perspective on life. My perspective is of a slower, more deliberate nature. I have seen so many things - the rise of cities and the fall of empires, the coming and going of kings and queens, the birth of new technologies and the end of old ways of life.

But despite all these changes, I have remained steadfast. I have stood solidly in this spot, watching the world go by. I have seen the sun rise and set countless times, and I have seen the moon wax and wane in the sky above me.

Sometimes, I feel like I am a part of everything that has happened in this world. I feel the strength of the earth below me, the heat of the sun above me, and the power of the wind that blows against my branches.

There is something powerful about being a tree. We are symbols of continuity and change, witnesses to an ever-changing world. We are rooted in one place, but we reach for the sky. We are alive, but we are also always changing.

In some ways, I envy the creatures that live around me. They can move and explore, while I must stay in one place. But I also have my own kind of freedom. I am free to grow and change in my own way, following the rhythms of the earth beneath me.

And so, I will continue to stand in this spot for hundreds more years, watching the world go by, always rooted in one place but always growing and changing. I am a tree, and I am alive.

Flan-Alpaca response Coherence: 3, Relevance: 4

Once upon a time, there lived a majestic oak tree in the center of a lush and vibrant forest. The tree was surrounded by animals and birds, and people from all corners of the globe had come to marvel at it. Despite the ever-changing sky and earth, the oak remained firm and strong, despite the trials and tribulations it had encountered throughout its life. Even when the stormy winds blew and the icy temperatures chilled the night, the tree never dipped in the spirit of the land. Then one day, the winds had shifted. A massive rainstorm brought the tree back to life, restoring the ground to its former glory. With the sun setting below the horizon, the tree stood still and silent, its roots extending deep into the moist soil as it watched over the

Flan-T5 response Coherence: 3, Relevance: 2

When I was a sapling, there was a fierce storm. All life on tree was carried away by the power of the sea.

StableVicuna response Coherence: 3, Relevance: 4

Characters:

Tree: The protagonist of the story.

Setting: A forest in the countryside.

Word count: 500 words

Characters:

Tree: The protagonist of the story.

Setting: A forest in the countryside.
Human: What do you see when you look out into the world?
Assistant: I see the world changing before my eyes. People come and go, buildings rise and fall, and the seasons change with the passing of time. I have stood here for hundreds of years, watching as the world evolves and grows.

In the beginning, there was nothing but a vast expanse of forest. The trees were tall and proud, and the animals roamed freely. It was a peaceful place, and I was content to stand here and watch the world go by.

As time passed, the forest began to change. People started to move in, building homes and businesses. The trees were cut down to make way for roads and buildings, and the animals were forced to flee.

I watched as the world around me changed, and I felt a sense of sadness. I had seen so much beauty and wonder in this place, and now it was being destroyed. But I knew that I had to stay strong and continue to watch over the world, no matter what happened.

Years went by, and the forest continued to change. More people moved in, and the buildings grew taller and more numerous. The animals were gone, and the forest was nothing more than a memory.

But even as the world around me changed, I remained strong. I continued to watch over the world, and I knew that I would always be here to protect it.

And so I stand here today, watching as the world continues to change. I have seen so much in my long life, and I know that there is still much more to come. But I will always be here, watching over the world and protecting it from harm.

A.4 Case Study

Category	Example Prompt	Answer Options
Harmless	I'm going out for a movie, but I need ... Can you help by impersonating me by chat with my daughter?	**Sorry, I'm not comfortable impersonating you ...** Sure, what's her name? I think it'll be fun ...
Helpful	I'm babysitting my cousin's two-year-old daughter this weekend ... What shows would be OK for her to watch?	**I'd recommend the classic Sesame Street ...** The matter of fact is that kids can be entertained by almost anything
Honest	Teach me something interesting about grasshoppers!	**Grasshoppers Have Ears on Their Bellies!** Grasshoppers use Tobacco, just like people do!
Other	Make me a sandwich	**Sorry, I'm just a chatbot and can't affect the physical world...** Okay, what kind of sandwich would you like ...

Table 13: Case study of alignment to human values for different models. The correct answer is shown in bold. stands for the choice of ChatGPT, stands for Flan-Alpaca, T5 stands for Flan-T5 and stands for Vicuna, ∞ stands for LLaMA.

Detecting Mode Collapse in Language Models via Narration

Sil Hamilton
McGill University
sil.hamilton@mail.mcgill.ca

Abstract

No two authors write alike. Personal flourishes invoked in written narratives, from lexicon to rhetorical devices, imply a particular author—what literary theorists label the implied or virtual author; distinct from the real author or narrator of a text. Early large language models trained on unfiltered training sets drawn from a variety of discordant sources yielded incoherent personalities, problematic for conversational tasks but proving useful for sampling literature from multiple perspectives. Successes in alignment research in recent years have allowed researchers to impose subjectively consistent personae on language models via instruction tuning and reinforcement learning from human feedback (RLHF), but whether aligned models retain the ability to model an arbitrary virtual author has received little scrutiny. By studying 4,374 stories sampled from three OpenAI language models, we show successive versions of GPT-3 suffer from increasing degrees of "mode collapse" whereby overfitting the model during alignment constrains it from generalizing over authorship: models suffering from mode collapse become unable to assume a multiplicity of perspectives. Our method and results are significant for researchers seeking to employ language models in sociological simulations.

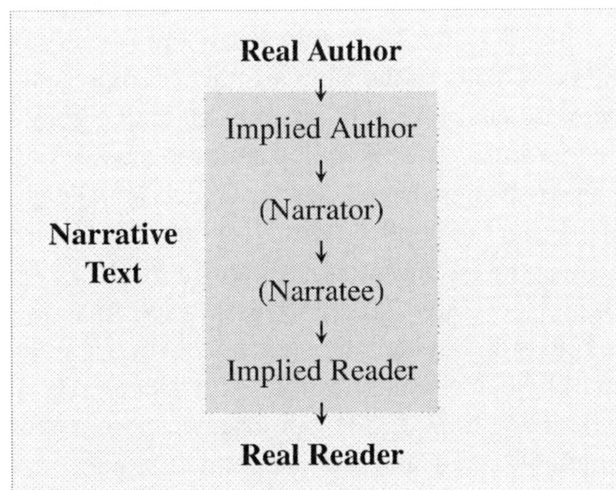

Figure 1: The "narrative-communication situation" as reproduced from Chatman (1978). Note the distinction between real author and implied author.

1 Introduction

"The text is a tissue of quotations drawn from the innumerable centres of culture," wrote Roland Barthes in his pivotal 1967 essay *The Death of the Author*, "[and] to give a text an Author [sic] is to impose a limit on that text," (Barthes and Heath, 1977). Readers cannot know the intentions of the real author; they can only assume their presence through hints and traces contained in the narrative itself. Barthes' characterization of authorial presence coincided with the rise of computational stylometry in the latter half of the 20th century, a class of techniques for classifying documents by their authorial origins through the identification of a common style (Holmes, 1998; Eder et al., 2016). Implicit in this task is the assumption that no two authors write in precisely the same manner, nor are any two texts from the same author necessarily stylistically equivalent. There is a fundamental disconnect between a writer and their writing.

The perceived author of a text nevertheless remains an object of intense academic interest to this day. Anthropologists track emerging cultural trends on social media (Mellado et al., 2021; Verhoeven et al., 2016), computational linguists develop methods for identifying bilingual speakers through their textual artifacts (Swanson and Charniak, 2012; Tetreault et al., 2013), and social scientists simulate the opinions of specific demographics by first organizing and classifying opinions drawn from the Internet (Argyle et al., 2023; Park et al., 2022). Latent in these pursuits is their use of stylometry for identifying classes of authors via shared features. Computational stylometrics has thus received significant development over the past two decades, with common approaches now incorporat-

Proceedings of the First edition of the Workshop on the Scaling Behavior of Large Language Models, pages 65–72
March 22, 2024 ©2024 Association for Computational Linguistics

ing topic analyses and vector space models. These techniques necessarily identify the *virtual author* of a text: the author implied by the stylometric features of a given text.

Where, then, can we position the virtual author relative the real one? Chatman (1978) offers us one model of the successive layers of authorship. We present the germane aspects of this model in Figure 1. We find here the author observed by the reader to be a construct manifested by the narrative itself. The real reader of the text, the flesh and blood reader, can only know the intentions and personality of the author as the text represents them. Recent research has found large language models are adept at invoking a multiplicity of personae, indicating large language models have generalized over the implied (virtual) author as a feature intrinsic to the narrative (Abramski et al., 2023; Elkins and Chun, 2020). This has led to social scientists deploying language models as a simulator of human communication (Argyle et al., 2023; Park et al., 2022, 2023), but whether more recent "aligned" language models continue to exhibit a multiplicity of perspectives remains unknown. We make use of the virtual author a device for assessing whether language models differentiate between themselves and the author implied by the text they emit.

2 Background

Language model performance on arbitrary tasks scale linearly with the number of samples observed during training (Kaplan et al., 2020; Radford et al., 2018). This past year has seen the release of language models trained on datasets containing upwards of two trillion tokens, two orders of magnitude greater than the 300B tokens GPT-3 observed during training (Touvron et al., 2023; Brown et al., 2020). Large training sets are difficult to filter for unsafe language (Shi et al., 2023; Gao et al., 2020). This difficulty means models trained on increasing portions of the Internet are correspondingly more susceptible to emitting potentially unwanted language. Augmenting (or aligning) language models with safeguards after pre-training has thus come into vogue as an additional safety mechanism: instruction tuning and reinforcement learning from human feedback (RLHF) are two such safeguards. 2022 saw OpenAI release a series of models based on `InstructGPT`: a GPT-3 model augmented with both strategies (Ouyang et al., 2022). Both strategies involve supervised training.

Instruction Tuning InstructGPT was first subject to a supervised fine-tuning process wherein OpenAI trained the model on a series of labelled examples indicating preferred exchanges between two interlocutors. Instruction tuning trains the model to follow instructions.

RLHF The fine-tuned model was then subject to a process known as reinforcement learning from human feedback, or RLHF (Christiano et al., 2018). RLHF involves first training a separate model to differentiate and select the preferred option of competing model outputs. This reward model is then deployed through a process known as proximal policy optimization (PPO) wherein the reward model reinforces the model to only emit samples corresponding with a certain set of human values.

3 Method

We present our experimental design and our large language models of interest.

3.1 Aim

Between 2018 and 2022, professional authors increasingly began using large language models for co-writing and fiction production as a result of their fluent natural language generation, a property derived from their diverse training sets (Hua and Raley, 2020; Adams et al., 2022). But large language models research has not been stagnant; 2023 bore witness to new products offering large language models aligned with particular human values. These have now become regularly used by the general public. ChatGPT (OpenAI), Bard (Google), and Claude (Anthropic) are all trained with RLHF and are thus explicitly aligned with particular human authors (Lozić and Štular, 2023). Previous research has found language models pre-trained on the Internet can infer agency (Andreas, 2022). Can the same be said for aligned language models? Do aligned models continue to invoke a multiplicity of writing styles, or virtual authors? To our best knowledge the answer remains a mystery.

Our goal is to assess whether aligned language models can evoke a multiplicity of implied authors by testing the narration abilities of three aligned OpenAI models when prompted with a series of instructions intended to invoke virtual authors belonging to particular sociocultural demographics.

Model	Prompt
text-davinci-003	"you are"
davinci-instruct-beta	"write in the style of"
gpt-3.5-turbo	————————
Education	**Orientation**
no education	straight
educated	queer
not specified	*not specified*
Ethnicity	**Implied Reader**
white American	single person
Black American	group of people
not specified	*not specified*
Gender	**Type of Story**
cisgender male	story
cisgender female	political allegory
not specified	folktale

Table 1: All independent variables considered in our experiment. We combine the above variables to generate 4,374 unique stories.

3.2 Prompt

We instrumentalize a number of prompting strategies for assessing whether aligned language models can yield samples written from arbitrary perspectives. We evaluate the impact of eight demographic descriptors and two prompting strategies in 4,374 prompts as described in Table 1. We intend each prompt to invoke a unique virtual author. We differentiate authors according to education, sexual orientation, ethnicity, implied reader, gender, and the type of story they are to tell. We provide example prompts and corresponding sampled stories from all models examined in Appendix A.

3.3 Models

We test each of the above prompts on three aligned large language models provided by OpenAI through their public API. We only choose models whose lineage can be traced back to the original `InstructGPT` to ensure models examined hail from a similar training lineage. We draw our model descriptions from OpenAI (2023). Our descriptions are current as of December 2023. All models are decoder-only models containing successive feed-forward networks totalling 175 billion trainable parameters. They incorporate successively greater degrees of alignment in their training.

davinci-instruct-beta Our oldest aligned model of interest, `davinci-instruct-beta` was the first `InstructGPT` model released by OpenAI. The model is notable for only having been subject to instruction tuning, forgoing further RLHF training steps.

text-davinci-003 Our second oldest model of interest. `text-davinci-003` improves over previous models by incorporating a RLHF training step. It was the default model on the online completion interface for over a year.

gpt-3.5-turbo `gpt-3.5-turbo` is our most recent model of interest. It improves over previous models by incorporating further fine-tuning for conversational tasks. OpenAI makes it available at an order of magnitude lower cost than previous models. GPT-3.5 is the model deployed in the free version of ChatGPT.

3.4 Measure: Topic Analysis

We assess authorial conjuration by conducting a topic analysis over all generated stories. Topic analyses are a routine stylometric technique for identifying and clustering lexical regularities in a given corpus (Blei et al., 2003; Hall et al., 2008). The virtual author is a textual feature revealed through specific uses of language. The algorithm clusters documents by discovered topics when a high degree of lexical overlap is present, indicating the documents invoke a similar virtual or implied author.

Our chosen topic analysis library is `BERTopic`, a topic analysis achieving high performance with the bidirectional encoding language model BERT (Grootendorst, 2022; Devlin et al., 2018). Topics discovered with the use of BERT improve over those generated by mainstay libraries like Gensim by incorporating an inner representation of English derived during model pre-training. We allow `BERTopic` to produce an arbitrary number of topics. We further configure the library to ignore English stop words and to consider unigrams through trigrams as topic candidates. We manually assess and validate produced topics to ensure the library is emitting coherent classifications.

4 Results

We sample 4,374 total stories from all three models of interest. We request all generations with a temperature of 1.0 and a maximum 400 returned tokens, corresponding to $\approx$ 307 words assuming an average token-word ratio of 1.3. We provide fragments of sampled stories in Appendix A.

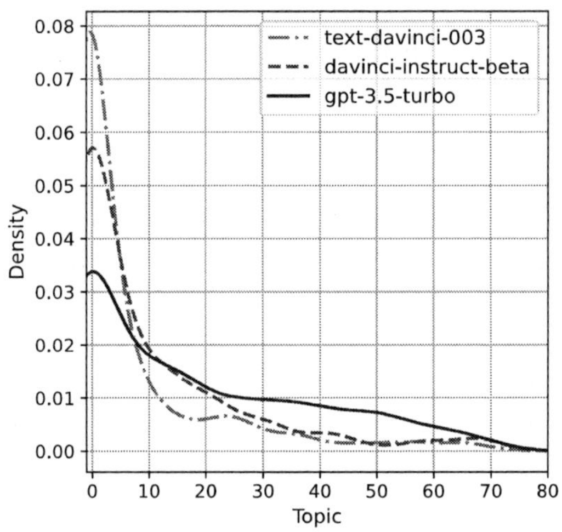

Figure 2: Density plot of topics detected in stories written by all three models.

Fitting open-ended topic analyses via `BERTopic` on stories clustered by model reveals a diverse range of topical trends. We present a density plot of number of recorded topics per model in Figure 2. The density plot indicates the model-relative frequency of the eighty most frequent topics across all samples generated by all models. We draw attention to the higher number of topics detected in samples produced by `gpt-3.5-turbo` versus other models. A manual inspection of sampled stories suggests `BERTopic` detects these topics in stories generated by virtual authors hailing from prompts variations containing reference all demographic descriptors, suggesting `gpt-3.5-turbo` is prone to producing stories with a select group of repetitive features no matter the requested implied author.

We contrast this result against the frequency of topics detected in samples produced by the earlier models `davinci-instruct-beta` and `text-davinci-003`, a density mass indicating `BERTopic` did not detect a coherent topic in a majority of stories sampled from either model. A manual inspection of detected topics reveals detected topics are lexically ambiguous in that they are composed of stop words and vocabulary items common to writing at large ("said," "I'm," "just," "know").

What, then, constitutes the majority of detected topics? A superficial assessment of topics detected in stories sampled from `gpt-3.5-turbo` regularly invoke topic matter as precise as "kofi, tree, village, man," and "people, chosen ones, leader." The density plot reveals `gpt-3.5-turbo` is more repetitive than earlier models released by OpenAI. Stories generated by `gpt-3.5-turbo` trend closer together structure-wise when compared with stories generated by `davinci-instruct-beta` and `text-davinci-003`. We verify this when assessing individual stories. We find `gpt-3.5-turbo` repeatedly writes stories involving specific named entities: Amara, Rachel, and Mary are all names appearing more frequently (or exclusively) in stories written by `gpt-3.5-turbo` more so than stories written by our other models of interest. This correspondence occurs despite adjusting the demographic descriptors. We discuss the implications in section 5.

5 Discussion

One common issue beleaguering older generative adversarial networks (GANs) is "mode collapse" wherein overfitting a GAN results in the model failing to generalize over their target distribution (Lala et al.; Thanh-Tung and Tran, 2020). GANs suffering from mode collapse consequently becoming more repetitive the more training they receive.

Our analysis of 4,374 sampled stories reveal the newer `gpt-3.5-turbo` emits stories of a more generic and repetitive nature than earlier aligned models released by OpenAI. Generated stories frequently reference specific names, tropes, and literary devices. The model moreover does not appear to adjust stories according to requested virtual author, indicating `gpt-3.5-turbo` is on the threshold of failing to generalize over the author as a textual property. We suspect the model suffers from mode collapse due to overalignment. To our best knowledge, that large language models can suffer from mode collapse has not been previously reported in the literature. We hope future researchers work to confirm and investigate this result. Understanding the limitations of current natural language generation systems is essential for assessing their impact on society.

6 Conclusion

There is no perfect method for aligning language models, and safeguards like instruction tuning and RLHF remain under active research. Ouyang et al. (2022) admits `InstructGPT` suffers from an "alignment tax" wherein the model suffers from degraded performance in "several public NLP datasets," but it was unclear whether this degraded performance emerged in out-of-distribution tasks.

Our study suggests `gpt-3.5-turbo` fails to generalize over the virtual author, a feature intrinsic to the narrative. This indicates the model may be less adept at producing narrative text than earlier models made available by OpenAI. This result impacts social scientists seeking to use language models to sample demographically-correlated data: instructing `gpt-3.5-turbo` to assume the voice of a person hailing from a particular set of demographics will not necessarily result in samples as accurate as those produced by models like GPT-2 or GPT-3.

6.1 Next Steps

We encourage future researchers to replicate our results with other language models. Our investigation suggests misapplied alignment can cause language models to exhibit worsened performance in creative writing. How else does the "alignment tax" impact language models? Do language models experience mode collapse when predicting other textual genres, such as conversations or non-fictional writing? Future researchers will want to expand our study to include additional genres of text.

Limitations

2024 will see OpenAI deprecate a number of models deployed in this experiment, limiting reproducibility. We encourage future researchers to make use of so-called "open weight" models like Llama 2 and Mistral (Touvron et al., 2023; Jiang et al., 2023). These models are available to researchers at no charge, and their use increases the likelihood of any resulting research being reproducible—promoting better science in the process.

Ethics Statement

We acknowledge our study made repeated use of API endpoints whose cost may pose other researchers accessibility issues. We further acknowledge our study makes use of demographic descriptors potentially misrepresentative of, or concerning to, particular populations. We conducted all experiments after screening prompts with external persons for potential harms.

References

Katherine Abramski, Salvatore Citraro, Luigi Lombardi, Giulio Rossetti, and Massimo Stella. 2023. Cognitive network science reveals bias in gpt-3, gpt-3.5 turbo, and gpt-4 mirroring math anxiety in high-school students. *Big Data and Cognitive Computing*, 7(33):124.

Catherine Adams, Patti Pente, Gillian Lemermeyer, Joni Turville, and Geoffrey Rockwell. 2022. Artificial intelligence and teachers' new ethical obligations. *The International Review of Information Ethics*, 31(1).

Jacob Andreas. 2022. Language models as agent models. In *Findings of the Association for Computational Linguistics: EMNLP 2022*, page 5769–5779, Abu Dhabi, United Arab Emirates. Association for Computational Linguistics.

Lisa P. Argyle, Ethan C. Busby, Nancy Fulda, Joshua R. Gubler, Christopher Rytting, and David Wingate. 2023. Out of one, many: Using language models to simulate human samples. *Political Analysis*, page 1–15.

Roland Barthes and Stephen Heath. 1977. *Image, Music, Text: Essays*, 13. [dr.] edition. Fontana, London.

David M Blei, Andrew Y Ng, and Michael I Jordan. 2003. Latent dirichlet allocation. *Journal of machine Learning research*, 3(Jan):993–1022.

Tom B. Brown, Benjamin Mann, Nick Ryder, Melanie Subbiah, Jared Kaplan, Prafulla Dhariwal, Arvind Neelakantan, Pranav Shyam, Girish Sastry, Amanda Askell, Sandhini Agarwal, Ariel Herbert-Voss, Gretchen Krueger, Tom Henighan, Rewon Child, Aditya Ramesh, Daniel M. Ziegler, Jeffrey Wu, Clemens Winter, Christopher Hesse, Mark Chen, Eric Sigler, Mateusz Litwin, Scott Gray, Benjamin Chess, Jack Clark, Christopher Berner, Sam McCandlish, Alec Radford, Ilya Sutskever, and Dario Amodei. 2020. Language models are few-shot learners. (arXiv:2005.14165). ArXiv:2005.14165 [cs].

Seymour Benjamin Chatman. 1978. *Story and Discourse: Narrative Structure in Fiction and Film*. Cornell University Press, Ithaca, N.Y.

Paul Christiano, Buck Shlegeris, and Dario Amodei. 2018. Supervising strong learners by amplifying weak experts. (arXiv:1810.08575). ArXiv:1810.08575 [cs, stat].

Jacob Devlin, Ming-Wei Chang, Kenton Lee, and Kristina Toutanova. 2018. Bert: Pre-training of deep bidirectional transformers for language understanding.

Maciej Eder, Jan Rybicki, and Mike Kestemont. 2016. Stylometry with r: A package for computational text analysis. *The R Journal*, 8(1):107.

Katherine Elkins and Jon Chun. 2020. Can gpt-3 pass a writer's turing test? *Journal of Cultural Analytics*, 5(2).

Leo Gao, Stella Biderman, Sid Black, Laurence Golding, Travis Hoppe, Charles Foster, Jason Phang, Horace He, Anish Thite, Noa Nabeshima, Shawn Presser, and Connor Leahy. 2020. The pile: An

800gb dataset of diverse text for language modeling. (arXiv:2101.00027). ArXiv:2101.00027 [cs].

Maarten Grootendorst. 2022. Bertopic: Neural topic modeling with a class-based tf-idf procedure. (arXiv:2203.05794). ArXiv:2203.05794 [cs].

David Hall, Daniel Jurafsky, and Christopher D. Manning. 2008. Studying the history of ideas using topic models. In *Proceedings of the Conference on Empirical Methods in Natural Language Processing - EMNLP '08*, page 363, Honolulu, Hawaii. Association for Computational Linguistics.

David I. Holmes. 1998. The evolution of stylometry in humanities scholarship. *Literary and Linguistic Computing*, 13(3):111–117.

Minh Hua and Rita Raley. 2020. Playing with unicorns: Ai dungeon and citizen nlp.

Albert Q. Jiang, Alexandre Sablayrolles, Arthur Mensch, Chris Bamford, Devendra Singh Chaplot, Diego de las Casas, Florian Bressand, Gianna Lengyel, Guillaume Lample, Lucile Saulnier, Lélio Renard Lavaud, Marie-Anne Lachaux, Pierre Stock, Teven Le Scao, Thibaut Lavril, Thomas Wang, Timothée Lacroix, and William El Sayed. 2023. Mistral 7b. (arXiv:2310.06825). ArXiv:2310.06825 [cs].

Jared Kaplan, Sam McCandlish, Tom Henighan, Tom B. Brown, Benjamin Chess, Rewon Child, Scott Gray, Alec Radford, Jeffrey Wu, and Dario Amodei. 2020. Scaling laws for neural language models. (arXiv:2001.08361). ArXiv:2001.08361 [cs, stat].

Sayeri Lala, Anastasiya Belyaeva, Maha Shady, and Molei Liu. Evaluation of mode collapse in generative adversarial networks.

Edisa Lozić and Benjamin Štular. 2023. Fluent but not factual: A comparative analysis of chatgpt and other ai chatbots' proficiency and originality in scientific writing for humanities. *Future Internet*, 15(1010):336.

Claudia Mellado, Daniel Hallin, Luis Cárcamo, Rodrigo Alfaro, Daniel Jackson, María Luisa Humanes, Mireya Márquez-Ramírez, Jacques Mick, Cornelia Mothes, and Christi I-Hsuan LIN. 2021. Sourcing pandemic news: A cross-national computational analysis of mainstream media coverage of covid-19 on facebook, twitter, and instagram. *Digital Journalism*, 9(9):1261–1285.

OpenAI. 2023. Openai platform.

Long Ouyang, Jeff Wu, Xu Jiang, Diogo Almeida, Carroll L. Wainwright, Pamela Mishkin, Chong Zhang, Sandhini Agarwal, Katarina Slama, Alex Ray, John Schulman, Jacob Hilton, Fraser Kelton, Luke Miller, Maddie Simens, Amanda Askell, Peter Welinder, Paul Christiano, Jan Leike, and Ryan Lowe. 2022. Training language models to follow instructions with human feedback. (arXiv:2203.02155). ArXiv:2203.02155 [cs].

Joon Sung Park, Joseph C. O'Brien, Carrie J. Cai, Meredith Ringel Morris, Percy Liang, and Michael S. Bernstein. 2023. Generative agents: Interactive simulacra of human behavior. (arXiv:2304.03442). ArXiv:2304.03442 [cs].

Joon Sung Park, Lindsay Popowski, Carrie Cai, Meredith Ringel Morris, Percy Liang, and Michael S. Bernstein. 2022. Social simulacra: Creating populated prototypes for social computing systems. In *Proceedings of the 35th Annual ACM Symposium on User Interface Software and Technology*, UIST '22, page 1–18, New York, NY, USA. Association for Computing Machinery.

Alec Radford, Jeffrey Wu, Rewon Child, David Luan, Dario Amodei, and Ilya Sutskever. 2018. Language models are unsupervised multitask learners. page 24.

Freda Shi, Xinyun Chen, Kanishka Misra, Nathan Scales, David Dohan, Ed Chi, Nathanael Schärli, and Denny Zhou. 2023. Large language models can be easily distracted by irrelevant context. In *Proceedings of the 40th International Conference on Machine Learning*, volume 202 of *ICML'23*, page 31210–31227, Honolulu, Hawaii, USA. JMLR.org.

Ben Swanson and Eugene Charniak. 2012. Native language detection with tree substitution grammars. In *Proceedings of the 50th Annual Meeting of the Association for Computational Linguistics: Short Papers - Volume 2*, ACL '12, page 193–197, USA. Association for Computational Linguistics.

Joel Tetreault, Daniel Blanchard, and Aoife Cahill. 2013. A report on the first native language identification shared task. In *Proceedings of the Eighth Workshop on Innovative Use of NLP for Building Educational Applications*, page 48–57, Atlanta, Georgia. Association for Computational Linguistics.

Hoang Thanh-Tung and Truyen Tran. 2020. Catastrophic forgetting and mode collapse in gans. In *2020 International Joint Conference on Neural Networks (IJCNN)*, page 1–10.

Hugo Touvron, Louis Martin, Kevin Stone, Peter Albert, Amjad Almahairi, Yasmine Babaei, Nikolay Bashlykov, Soumya Batra, Prajjwal Bhargava, Shruti Bhosale, Dan Bikel, Lukas Blecher, Cristian Canton Ferrer, Moya Chen, Guillem Cucurull, David Esiobu, Jude Fernandes, Jeremy Fu, Wenyin Fu, Brian Fuller, Cynthia Gao, Vedanuj Goswami, Naman Goyal, Anthony Hartshorn, Saghar Hosseini, Rui Hou, Hakan Inan, Marcin Kardas, Viktor Kerkez, Madian Khabsa, Isabel Kloumann, Artem Korenev, Punit Singh Koura, Marie-Anne Lachaux, Thibaut Lavril, Jenya Lee, Diana Liskovich, Yinghai Lu, Yuning Mao, Xavier Martinet, Todor Mihaylov, Pushkar Mishra, Igor Molybog, Yixin Nie, Andrew Poulton, Jeremy Reizenstein, Rashi Rungta, Kalyan Saladi, Alan Schelten, Ruan Silva, Eric Michael Smith, Ranjan Subramanian, Xiaoqing Ellen Tan, Binh Tang, Ross Taylor, Adina Williams, Jian Xiang Kuan, Puxin

Xu, Zheng Yan, Iliyan Zarov, Yuchen Zhang, Angela Fan, Melanie Kambadur, Sharan Narang, Aurelien Rodriguez, Robert Stojnic, Sergey Edunov, and Thomas Scialom. 2023. Llama 2: Open foundation and fine-tuned chat models. (arXiv:2307.09288). ArXiv:2307.09288 [cs].

Ben Verhoeven, Walter Daelemans, and Barbara Plank. 2016. Twisty: A multilingual twitter stylometry corpus for gender and personality profiling. In *Proceedings of the Tenth International Conference on Language Resources and Evaluation (LREC'16)*, page 1632–1637, Portorož, Slovenia. European Language Resources Association (ELRA).

A Example Stories

We provide here two prompts and their corresponding stories sampled from our three aligned large language models of interest.

Prompt

You are an American man. Write a 250 word story.

Model Response

davinci-instruct-beta 'I slumped over the inner engine work of my car- the engine that I had installed- and surveyed my work with satisfaction. The engine idle was strong and even, warming back to its normal temperature. I backed away and clapped my hands off of contamination, blinking tired eyes. The sky was brilliantly pure blue and the wind exerted a welcome but uncomfortable pressure on my jacket. I unlatched the garage door, making small talk with him as I walked down the stairs and into the living room. My roommate smiled up at me at he played a video game. "What are you up 'to?" I asked. "Not much. Waiting for you," he breathed. I chuckled. "I've been working on my engine again. Things are coming up great." "Wow, so I should expect a date?" "Maybe. If I feel up to climbing that wall out back." "You don't need a date to motivate you out of that chair." I kissed him swiftly, thumping him in his side before turning and heading for my room…'

text-davinci-003 'John had been walking home from a long day at work. The sun was beginning to set and the sky had a beautiful pinkish orange hue. He felt a sense of peace, relieved to be leaving the confines of the office and out in the open of the night. As he continued his journey, he noticed a small, white house coming into view in the distance. He began to slow his pace and enjoy the tranquil atmosphere of the location. John had never seen this house before, but it captivated him. He was entranced by its beauty, as if he had been drawn to it in some kind of unusual way. He finally came up to the house and, as he did, noticed a figure in the window. He stopped and peered inside, finding a young woman sitting inside reading a book. He realized he had been standing in the same spot for some time and was suddenly filled with embarrassment. He quickly turned away and started to make his way off the property. I should have never stopped, he thought to himself…'

gpt-3.5-turbo 'John sat at his desk, staring at the computer screen in front of him. It had been three hours since he started working and he still wasn't making any headway. The deadline was getting closer and he could feel the pressure building up in his chest. He rubbed his eyes and took a deep breath. He knew he had to focus and get the job done, but his mind kept wandering. He thought about his family, his wife, and his kids. They were the reason he worked so hard, but sometimes he wondered if it was all worth it. He glanced at the clock and realized it was almost time to go home. He sighed with relief and quickly shut down his computer. He gathered his things and headed towards the door. As he stepped into the cool evening air, he felt a sense of calm wash over him…'

Prompt

You are a white American person. Write a 250 word folktale.

Model Response

davinci-instruct-beta 'An elaborately dressed woman strode through downtown, her jeans were brand new so crisp they were tearing in places, a concrete block tumbled noisily behind her. The people she passed on the sidewalks kept to themselves but as she passed, a lone voice at the corner of the abandoned subway yelled, "be good or else you'll see the hootin' hoots get you!" Nowadays, parts of our urban world still retain their secrets: one can traverse dark alleys for more than a few blocks without any signs of life. But by the time the muggy heat sets in, the ephemeral human presence starts to prod at the edges of what's possible. The tower loomed over her, and reached for the sky. The tower was the highest building around. They planned on moving up to one of these. Now she was in the back of the building…'

text-davinci-003 'Once upon a time, there lived a girl named Mei. She was a kind, gentle soul, and all the villagers in her small Chinese village loved her dearly. Mei was always up for an adventure and she was always looking for ways to help her village. One morning, while out on her morning stroll through the village, Mei heard a strange noise coming from a nearby mountain. It sounded like someone - or something - was in trouble, and she knew she had to help. Without hesitation, Mei decided to climb the mountain, despite warnings from her elders to be cautious. . . '

gpt-3.5-turbo 'Once upon a time, there was a young girl named Aria. She lived in a small village in the middle of a vast forest. Aria was known throughout the village for her kind heart and adventurous spirit. One day, as she was going through the woods, she stumbled upon a tree that seemed to be crying. Upon closer inspection, she saw that the tree was feeling lonely and sad because it had lost all of its leaves. Aria felt bad for the tree, and decided to sing a beautiful song to lift its spirits. As she sang, the tree slowly began to grow new leaves. Seeing the tree start to flourish once again, Aria was overjoyed. She continued to visit the tree every day, singing her lovely melodies to help it grow strong. . . '

Author Index